EXPOSING THE DARKNESS

By Terry Board

© Burnett Publishing Company

Production and publication

By

Create Space

2016

Preface

As the situation of our world has been spiraling out of control, I felt compelled to write this book. These are controversies that bring about strong emotions in people. I wanted to get clear information out for the reader that perhaps hasn't had the time to do research. This book unfolds at the conception of our nation and it concludes right up until today. My desire is to unite people of like mind to join together and those who are not of the same mindset to come together and find truth. We are all seeking peace and are going about it in different ways. I hope true love; joy and peace will leap off the pages and enter your hearts. Yes there is a higher power and His name is Yahweh! Take a little time out of your life to read this book and find the truth you are desperately seeking for. If it doesn't transform you, wait a few days and throw the book away. This book scans through time and reaches out to all people, all faiths and all belief systems. I hope to one day hear from you and hear about your experience.

Terry

I want to say a special thank you to Lin McDowell for all the hours of listening to me read this book. Thank you, Janelle Young for editing. Kelly Leimer, Barbara Johnson and Linda Cesena I thank you for your prayers.

EXPOSING THE DARKNESS

Table of Contents

Histories of the Settlers	1-5
First 13 Colonies and President's Information	6-16
Slavery and its Ugliness	16-20
Separation of Church and State Debunked	21-23
The Constitution of the United States	23-72
Abortion: The Ultimate Murder	73-75
Secret Societies and Terrorism	76-80
Wars and Rumors of Wars	81-83
The Most Essential Election Ever	84-85
Modern Day Sodom and Gomorrah	86-87
All Lives Matter	88
Summary	89-91
Works Cited	92-93
Addendums Quotes	94

EXPOSING THE DARKNESS

It doesn't do any good to expose the darkness, if there is never a change. Exposure means to make known something secret. Ephesians 5:11 says, *"Take no part in unfruitful works of darkness, but instead expose them."* When you do expose those unfruitful works of darkness make sure you have all the facts and you are not taking part in them.

History of the Settlers

We must travel back in time to the reason men chose to leave their homes in search of a new world.

Christopher Columbus was the discoverer of America in 1492. The people were being told how they should worship God, and they were not free to worship as they wished. The pilgrim's came from far and wide to get to a land where they could be free. Many died before they could get there. The pilgrim's had to work hard and labor, day and night, to build shacks to live in and to be able to eat, and to keep their families healthy. They had no running water, no toilets, no showers, no electricity or any of the comforts we share today. The men in the colonies got together to write laws that every American could agree with. They were so far ahead of their time in choosing how to govern a free people. They were making it better for people to live and to protect themselves from those who would lie and cheat. You may be thinking how does this have anything to do with exposing the darkness? Stay with me throughout this book you will find facts that will expose the darkness, and its purpose is to bring all things to light. To make this Nation Great Again!

There were only 1 or 2 doctors available at this time of settling in the new nation. The pilgrims were dying right and left of scurvy. There were certainly not enough doctors around to help them. Then other doctors began to arrive later. Here is the history of the first doctor in America.

אֵל עוֹלָם

The history of the doctors in America commences with early physicians of the North American colonies.

With but little hope of material reward –sharing in every danger, hardship and privation of the other emigrants – a number of medical men of eminence came to the New World during formative days of the colonies; and the treatment and care which the settlers received at their hands were on a par with that administered to the friends and relatives whom they had left behind in their native lands.

Dr. Thomas Wooten was undoubtedly the progenitor of medicine in North America. Carrying a commission as Surgeon-General of the London Company, he arrived in 1607 on one of three ships bearing 165 colonists who landed at the mouth of the James River in Virginia, is named in honor of King James I, son of Mary Stuart who succeeded her half-sister, Elizabeth, upon the English throne.

The settlement of Jamestown was built. After their cherished dreams of finding gold had faded, these settlers turned their attention to the rich Virginia soil which was particularly adapted to the cultivation of two plants which were to determine the colony's future-tobacco and cotton.

During the following year, a Dr. Russel was accompanying Captain John Smith on his exploration of Chesapeake Bay.

But it would seem that neither of these physicians remained very long; because, in 1609, the hardy old warrior who had been the leader and protector to the first white settlement in the New World, after being wounded was compelled to return to England for lack of medical aid in the settlements.

In 1611, Dr. Lawrence Bohun succeeded Dr. Wooten as Physician-General of Virginia.

When Peter Minuit purchased the island of Manhattan for twenty four dollars in 1626, there was probably no physician in his party.

The first records of a doctor in New York-then New Amsterdam, are of one Johannes La Montagne, a Huguenot who arrived in 1637, and Dr. Herman Van den Bogaerdt.

Dr. La Montagne was counselor to the Director General of New Netherlands. Both of these men recorded to have possessed great learning.
The First Doctors in America   (**History of medicine.com**) #1

After a very short while the settlers ran into more trouble, hence The American Indian. The Indians were afraid of the White men and the White men were afraid of the Indians. In England they had heard of people on the Island that were considered savages. Of course there were a few battles until each could come to an agreement that they may be able to live together. Most Americans that have learned any history know of the story of Squanto. There are many other stories of how they began to live together peacefully and even shared the first Thanksgiving celebration together. They began arriving upon several shores Cape Cod, Roanoke Virginia, and Plymouth Massachusetts, for a start. The new land was soon given a name it was called New England.

אֶל עוֹלָם

When the Pilgrims first encountered the Native Americans during their early explorations of Cape Cod, both groups feared each other. There were nights when the Pilgrims could hear the noise of Indian drams, which made the Pilgrims uneasy about their neighbors. From the accounts they had heard from other explorers, they had come to think of the Indians as savages. They had no way of knowing that an Indian named Squanto was an English-speaking native who would befriend them and act as an interpreter between them and the Wampanoag Indians.

Literally, Wampanoag means "People of the Light." They are sometimes referred to as "Eastern People" since the first light each day appears in the east.

The Pilgrims' first winter in America was difficult. They lacked food, and about half of the

colonists had died of the "great sickness" during the first terrible winter.

In the spring, an Indian named Samoset entered the Plymouth Colony and introduced himself to the Pilgrims. Samoset had also been kidnapped by explorers and taken to England where he had learned the language. Samoset was an Abnaki Indian from Maine.

Later he returned with Squanto. Squanto was born about 1585 near what is now known as Plymouth, Massachusetts. He was a Pawtuxet Indian who was captured in 1614 by English seamen and taken to Spain where he was sold as a slave. Squanto escaped to England, where he lived for several years and learned to speak English.

In 1619, Squanto returned to his home and found most of the people of his tribe had died of disease. He joined the Wampanoags who were living near Plymouth, and in 1621, he met the Pilgrims. It was Squanto who would teach the Pilgrims how to find herring, a kind of fish, and to use it as a fertilizer when planting corn, pumpkins and beans. This was especially important to the Pilgrims because the seeds they had brought with them from England did not do well in the New England soil. Squanto also showed them how to find clams and eels in the rivers and how to hunt for deer, bears and turkeys. The children also learned where to find nuts and berries of all kinds.

© **Duane A. Cline 1999 The Pilgrims and Plymouth colony Rootsweb.ancestory.com**   #2

אֵל עוֹלָם

Without New England the history of the United States would have followed a very different pattern. This being so, we may well enquire what gave New England so distinctive and influential a part in the development of the American nation, and beyond all doubt the answer is — **the Christian Faith!**. Over a period of twelve years, in about 198 ships, men and their families arrived in Massachusetts Bay. They included gentlemen, merchants, farmers, craftsmen and ministers of the gospel. **The one thing which the vast majority possessed in common was a fervent commitment to the Word of God and to the gospel of the Lord Jesus Christ.**
(National Humanities Center)   #3

אֵל עוֹלָם

The Jamestown settlement, established in 1607, was the seat of England's first permanent colony in North America. After the failure of the Roanoke colonies, investors in the Virginia Company of London were anxious to find profit farther to the north, and in April 1607 three ships of settlers arrived at the Chesapeake Bay. The enterprise, fraught with disease, dissension, and determined Indian resistance, was a miserable failure at first.
(Encyclopedia Virginia)   #4

4

They settler's still belonged to the Church of England, and were bound to their rules. The whole reason for coming to a new land was to establish the freedom for each person to worship as they saw fit, and to develop a nation of **The Christian Faith**! They didn't want a dictator telling them how to live, worship, work, or own their own property. Among the first settlers to land in America were the ones who landed in Jamestown Virginia in 1607 and then 1620 Plymouth, Massachusetts, they came to the New World to escape religious persecution.

By 1770, more than 2 million people lived and worked in Great Britain's thirteen North American colonies. Are you familiar with whom and where those (13) colonies were?

First 13 Colonies and Presidential Information

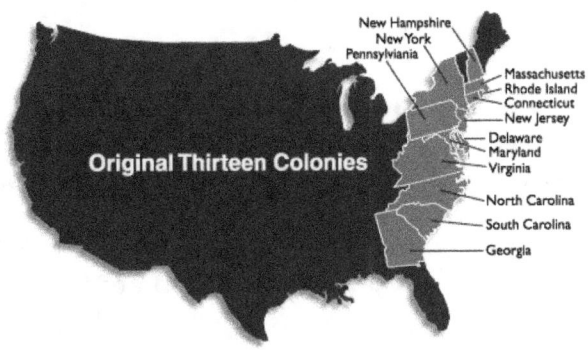

1. New Hampshire,

2. Massachusetts,

3. Connecticut,

4. Rhode Island,

5. New York,

6. New Jersey,

7. Pennsylvania,

8. Delaware,

9. Maryland,

10. Virginia,

11. North Carolina,

12. South Carolina

13 Georgia

These colonies were being established by England to serve as business ventures, so that they could acquire the goods raised here. I imagine the new settlers were a little perturbed that they came all this way, lost much of their families, were very ill and still were connected to England. By way of the framers of the constitution they set out to name this country after the first man that they had discovered it and so we became a new nation under God named America.

Now let's fast forward to the first President of The United States. Eleven states were part of the colonies prior to George Washington's Presidency. There were sixteen states in the Union during his first term in office.

This was our beloved George Washington

By the time Eisenhower, our 34th president took office; there were 50 States in the Union. In the beginning only land owners were allowed to vote. Women or blacks or poor people who didn't own property were not allowed to vote. I am assuming that it was a good thing because it kept elections in check by the most knowledgeable people. Then later women thought they should be allowed to vote hence, the women's suffrage act was enacted, June 14th 1919.

אֵל עוֹלָם

Grover Cleveland had to deal head on with a scandal while he was running for president in 1884. It was revealed that he had previously had an affair with a widow named Maria C. Halpin who had given birth to a son. She claimed that Cleveland was the father and named him Oscar Folsom Cleveland. Cleveland agreed to pay child support and then paid to put the child in an orphanage when

Halpin was no longer fit to raise him. This issue was brought forth during his 1884 campaign and became a chant "Ma, Ma, where's my Pa?" "Gone to the White House, ha, ha, ha!" However, Cleveland was honest about the entire affair which helped rather than hurt him, and he won the election.

Warren G. Harding's presidency was struck by many scandals. The Teapot Dome scandal was the most significant. In this, Albert Fall, Harding's Secretary of the Interior, sold the right to the oil reserves in Teapot Dome, Wyoming, and other locations in exchange for personal profit and cattle. He was eventually caught, convicted and sentenced to jail.

Watergate has become synonymous with presidential scandal. In 1972, five men were caught breaking into the Democratic National Headquarters located at the Watergate business complex. As the investigation into this and the break-in at Daniel Ellsberg's psychiatrist's office (Ellsberg had published the secret Pentagon Papers) developed, Richard Nixon and his advisors worked to cover-up the crimes. He would have surely been impeached but he did the right thing and resigned instead on August 9, 1974

Bill Clinton was implicated in a couple of scandals; the most significant for his presidency was the Monica Lewinsky affair. Lewinsky was a White House intern with whom Clinton had an intimate relationship, or as he later put it, an "improper physical relationship." He had previously denied this while giving a deposition in another case which resulted in a vote to impeach him by the House of Representatives in 1998. The Senate did not vote to remove him from office, but the event did mar his presidency as he joined Andrew Johnson as only the second president to be impeached.

In 1974, Hillary Clinton became a member of the presidential impeachment inquiry staff during the Watergate scandal. President Richard Nixon resigned later that year.

Hillary Clinton was once a Republican, even campaigning for Barry Goldwater in 1964.

She is also, according to author Sally Bedell Smith, the first presidential spouse to be subpoenaed. Bill and Hillary Clinton are the first and only first couple to be fingerprinted by the FBI.

http://americanhistory.about.com/od/uspresidents/tp/presidential_scandals.htm #5

Clinton Mafia

Clinton Mafia by Charles Krauthammer:
Charles Krauthammer on Hillary Clinton:

אֶל עוֹלָם

Recently, Charles Krauthammer alluded that he had no doubt some of the 30k Emails Hillary deleted from her private e-mail server very likely had References to the Clinton Foundation, which would be illegal and a conflict of interest.
The Clinton Foundation is organized crime" at its finest. Here is a good, concise summary of how the Clinton Foundation works as a tax free international money laundering scheme. It may eventually prove to be the largest political criminal enterprise in U.S. History.

This is a textbook case on how you hide foreign money sent to you and repackage it to be used for your own purposes. All tax free.

Here's how it works:
1. You create a separate foreign "charity." In this case, the Clintons set it up in Canada.
2. Foreign oligarchs and governments, then donate to this Canadian charity. In this case, over 1,000 did contributing mega millions. I'm sure they did this out of the goodness of their hearts, and expected nothing in return. (Imagine Putin's buddies waking up one morning and just deciding to send untold Million's to a Canadian charity)
3. The Canadian charity then bundles these separate donations and makes a massive donation to the Clinton Foundation.
4. The Clinton Foundation and the cooperating Canadian charity claim Canadian law prohibits the identification of individual donors.

5. The Clinton Foundation then "spends" some of this money for legitimate good works programs. Unfortunately, experts believe this is on the order of 10%. Much of the balance goes to enrich the Clintons, pay salaries to untold numbers of hangers on, and fund lavish travel, etc. Again, virtually tax free, which means you and I are subsidizing it.

6. The Clinton Foundation, with access to the world's best accountants, somehow fails to report much of this on their tax filings. They discover these "clerical errors" and begin the process of re-filing 5 years of tax returns.

7. Net result foreign money goes into the Clinton's pockets tax free and untraceable back to the original donor. This is the textbook definition of money laundering. Oh, by the way, the Canadian "charity" includes as a principal one Frank Giustra. (Google him.) He is the guy who was central to the formation of Uranium One, the Canadian company that somehow acquired massive U.S. Uranium interests and then sold them to an organization controlled by Russia. This transaction required U.S. State Department approval, and guess who was Secretary of State when the approval was granted.

As an aside, imagine how former Virginia Governor Bob McDonnell feels. That poor schlep is in jail because he and his wife took $165,000 in gifts and loans for doing minor favors for a guy promoting a vitamin company. Not legal but not exactly putting U.S. Security at risk.

Sarcasm aside, if you're still not persuaded this was a cleverly structured way to get unidentified foreign money to the Clintons, ask yourself this: Why did these foreign interests funnel money through a Canadian charity? Why not donate directly to the Clinton Foundation? Better yet, why not donate money directly to the people, organizations and countries in need?
This is the essence of money laundering and influence peddling. Now you know why Hillary's destruction of 30,000 e-mails was a risk she was willing to take. Bill and Hillary are devious, unprincipled, dishonest and criminal and they are Slick!

Warning: They could be back in the White House in January 2017. Don't let it happen.
Clinton Mafia by Charles Krauthammer #6

Secret Service agents: Hillary is a nightmare to work with

By Deroy Murdock October 2, 2015 | 8:50pm

"Good morning, ma'am," a member of the uniformed Secret Service once greeted Hillary Clinton.

"---- off," she replied.

That exchange is one among many that active and retired Secret Service agents shared with **Ronald Kessler, author of "First Family Detail,"** a compelling look at the intrepid personnel who shield America's presidents and their families — and those whom they guard.

Kessler writes flatteringly and critically about people in both parties. Regarding the Clintons, Kessler presents Chelsea as a model **protectee** who respected and appreciated her agents. He describes Bill as a difficult chief executive but an easygoing ex-president. And Kessler exposes Hillary as an epically abusive Arctic monster.

"When in public, Hillary smiles and acts graciously," Kessler explains. "As soon as the cameras are gone, her angry personality, nastiness, and imperiousness become evident."

He adds: "Hillary Clinton can make Richard Nixon look like Mahatma Gandhi."

Kessler was an investigative reporter with the Wall Street Journal and Washington Post and has penned 19 other books. Among much more in "First Family Detail," he reports:

- "Hillary was very rude to agents, and she didn't appear to like law enforcement or the military," former Secret Service agent Lloyd Bulman recalls. "She wouldn't go over and meet military people or police officers, as most protectees do. She was just really rude to almost everybody. She'd act like she didn't want you around, like you were beneath her."

11

"Hillary didn't like the military aides wearing their uniforms around the White House," one former agent remembers. "She asked if they would wear business suits instead. The uniform's a sign of pride, and they're proud to wear their uniform. I know that the military was actually really offended by it."

- Former agent Jeff Crane says, "Hillary would cuss at Secret Service drivers for going over bumps." Another former member of her detail recollects, "Hillary never talked to us ... Most all members of first families would talk to us and smile. She never did that."

"We spent years with her," yet another Secret Service agent notes. "She never said thank you."

- Within the White House, Hillary had a "standing rule that no one spoke to her when she was going from one location to another," says former FBI agent Coy Copeland. "In fact, anyone who would see her coming would just step into the first available office."

One former Secret Service agent states, "If Hillary was walking down a hall, you were supposed to hide behind drapes used as partitions."

- Hillary one day ran into a White House electrician who was changing a light bulb in the upstairs family quarters. She screamed at him, because she had demanded that all repairs be performed while the Clintons were outside the Executive Mansion.

"She caught the guy on a ladder doing the light bulb," says Franette McCulloch, who served at that time as assistant White House pastry chef. "He was a basket case."

- White House usher Christopher B. Emery unwisely called back Barbara Bush after she phoned him for computer troubleshooting. Emery helped the former first lady twice. Consequently, Kessler reports, Hillary sacked him. The father of four stayed jobless for a year.
- While running for US Senate, Hillary stopped at an upstate New York 4-H Club. As one Secret Service agent says, Hillary saw farmers and cows and then erupted. "She turned to a staffer and said, 'What the f--- did we come here for? There's no money here.'"

12

Secret Service "agents consider being assigned to her detail a form of punishment," Kessler concludes. "In fact, agents say being on Hillary Clinton's detail is the worst duty assignment in the Secret Service."

After studying the Secret Service and its relationships with dozens of presidents, vice presidents and their families, Ronald Kessler's astonishment at Hillary Clinton's inhumanity should reverberate in every American's head.

As he told me: "No one would hire such a person to work at a McDonald's, and yet she is being considered for president of the United States."

By Deroy Murdock October 2, 2015 | 8:50pm   #7

Deroy Murdock is a Fox News contributor.

Below is a list of all the American Presidents for those of you who do not know who they were and who they are now:
18th Century

1. George Washington
2. John Adams
19th Century

3. Thomas Jefferson
4. James Madison
5. James Monroe
6. John Quincy Adams
7. Andrew Jackson
8. Martin Van Buren
9. William Henry Harrison
10. John Tyler
11. James K. Polk
12. Zachary Taylor
13. Millard Fillmore
14. Franklin Pierce

15. James Buchanan
16. Abraham Lincoln
17. Andrew Johnson
18. Ulysses S. Grant
19. Rutherford B. Hayes
20. James Garfield
21. Chester A. Arthur
22. Grover Cleveland

13

23. Benjamin Harrison
24. Grover Cleveland
25. William McKinley
20th Century

26. Theodore Roosevelt
27. William Howard Taft
28. Woodrow Wilson
29. Warren G. Harding
30. Calvin Coolidge
31. Herbert Hoover
32. Franklin D. Roosevelt
33. Harry S. Truman
34. Dwight D. Eisenhower
35. John F. Kennedy
36. Lyndon B. Johnson
37. Richard M. Nixon
38. Gerald R. Ford
39. James Carter
40. Ronald Reagan
41. George H. W. Bush
42. William J. Clinton
21st Century

43. George W. Bush
44. Barack Obama
I don't mean to make you dizzy jumping around, but I'm now going to fast forward to today. In a little less than (2) months, we will be holding an election for President of the United States. For sixteen years we have had scandal and much disrespect for the highest office of these United States I believe ever! Ok I'm going to jump right in.

Hillary Insults American's that support her opponent by labeling them as a "Basket of Deplorable's"... she wants to rule the deplorables. You are less if you don't support her ways! Bill Clinton Insults "Make America great again"... Calls Donald Trump a racist for saying it ... Yet he said it when he was in office numerous times. Both of the Clintons spout out their mouths double standards continuously.

As I recall it was the Clinton era that started the whole political correctness. It was during their tenure that their drunkenness for power prevailed to change an entire nation to their despicable way of thinking. We had eight long years of their tyranny. They killed their way to the governorship in Arkansas and then to the White House [according to Clinton Chronicles by Jeremiah Films] and they want us to suck down some more of the venomous political correctness. Would you just listen to those words! (Political Correctness) Correctness: **To scold or punish so as to improve or reform. Conforming to standards; proper: *correct behavior.*** Now the definition is to make better, NOT to make us the way they want...That is the difference here! They want to correct us, to reform us! If you recall, Hitler wanted to reform the world to his evil ways of thinking. This definition of reform is the true definition, **Reform: To induce or persuade (a person) to give up <u>harmful</u> or <u>immoral practices</u>; cause to adopt a better way of life. Action to improve or correct what is wrong or defective in something: *health care reform.*** Get it, we are wrong and we need correction! Also I found it interesting that the dictionary would give an end to that definition by mentioning *health care reform.* Dear God what is wrong with YOU America? Everything worked well up until evil took over.

Yes, call it what it is people! We are living in very evil times. Yes, Mrs. Clinton you heard right I said EVIL!

There is even some speculation as to whether she is even still alive. Believe it or not the farfetched idea that there could be one or more body doubles for her. As I put two videos together and looked at them, I myself noticed a few things. In an old video of the real Hillary she has crow's feet and a wrinkled neck. In the one several nights ago I zoomed in and this person had NO neck wrinkles or NO sign of crow's feet. Also the woman who came out of Chelsea's apartment was much slimmer in the waste than Hillary.

אֵל עוֹלָם

Isaiah 20,21&23,24 *(20)* Woe to those who call evil good, and good evil; Who substitute darkness for light and light for darkness; Who substitute bitter for sweet and sweet for bitter! *(21)* Woe to those who are wise in their own eyes and clever in their own sight! *(23)* Who justify the wicked for a bribe, and take away the rights of the ones who are in the right! *(24)* Therefore, as a tongue of fire consumes stubble and dry grass collapses into the flame, so their root will become like rot and their blossom blow away as dust; for they have rejected the law of the LORD of hosts and despised the word of the Holy One of Israel. **NAS** #8

This great nation has moved into a political lethargy. We have set back on our laurels and let groups of people change our great nation and have done nothing to get it back. We need to <u>stand</u> up and speak out and fast for God to move our nation back to Him.

אֵל עוֹלָם

II Chronicles 7:14 **"If my people** (who? Christians) **who are called by my name will humble themselves, and pray** (He is not talking to the people that are <u>not</u> called by His name. He's talking to the ones called by His name) **and seek my face, turn from their wicked ways** (whose wicked ways? the Christians) **then will I hear from heaven, forgive their sin and heal their land!** This is God speaking folks! WE MUST LISTEN AND OBEY! **NAS** #9

Slavery and its Ugliness

I'm going to back track for a few minutes to 1619 and 1865, where they were now into full blown slavery. It first started with blacks and poor whites being slaves. Then it slowly evolved to only blacks who were thought of as chattel. Thank God for a man named Newton Knight who joined forces with the black man and fought against both sides in the war to free the slaves, and they wanted to become their own nation called The Free State of Jones. He himself married a black woman, and they owned a plantation.

אֶל עוֹלָם

After 1619, when a Dutch ship brought 20 Africans ashore at the British colony of Jamestown, Virginia, slavery spread throughout the American colonies. Though it is impossible to give accurate figures, some historians have estimated that 6 to 7 million slaves were imported to the New World during the 18th century alone, depriving the African continent of some of its healthiest and ablest men and women. Lincoln issued a preliminary emancipation proclamation, and on January 1, 1863, he made it official that "slaves within any State, or designated part of a State...in rebellion, shall be then, thenceforward, and forever free." **(History.com)** #10

אֶל עוֹלָם

By April 1865 the Confederate rebellion had been crushed and the American Civil War was finally over. Mississippi was occupied by Federal troops sent to maintain order and to protect the civil rights of former slaves. Captain Newt Knight was called into service by the United States Army as a commissioner in charge of distributing thousands of pounds of food to the poor and starving people in the Jones County area. Newt was also sent to rescue several black children who were still being held in slavery in Smith County.

From 1867-1876, Mississippi was under <u>*Radical Reconstruction*</u> *to protect the civil rights of black citizens. More than 200 blacks were elected to local, state, and federal offices in Mississippi as members of the Republican Party. However, political equality would soon be challenged by the*

__Democratic Party__ and by __terrorist groups__ such as the Ku Klux Klan. At great personal danger, Newt Knight became a strong supporter of the Republican Party. In 1872, he was appointed as a deputy U.S. Marshal for the Southern District to help maintain the fragile democracy.

In the statewide elections of 1875, however, violence and __election fraud__ (sound familiar?) kept most blacks and Republicans from voting. Democratic candidates committed to "white rule" were swept into office. White terrorists shot out the windows of the Governor's Mansion to intimidate Republican <u>Governor Adelbert Ames</u>. Ames pleaded for federal troops to help keep order, but President Ulysses S. Grant refused. Governor Ames tried organizing a state militia to protect the voting process. In 1875, he appointed __Newt Knight__ as Colonel of the First Regiment Infantry of Jasper County. But the tide had already turned against Republican rule in Mississippi, and Governor Ames was forced to resign. He lamented that blacks "are to be returned to a condition of serfdom — an era of second slavery." Blacks could not vote freely in Mississippi again for nearly 100 years.

Newt retreated to his farm in Jasper County after 1875 and brought his wartime ally, the former slave Rachel, with him. His white wife, Serena, soon left and Newt and Rachel were married. She bore him several children. Newt faced danger for living openly with a black woman. But, as he liked to say, "There's [sic] a lots of ways I'd ruther __[rather]__[sic] die than be scared to death." Newton Knight died February 16, 1922, of natural causes at age 85. Under the Mississippi Constitution of 1890, it was a crime for whites and blacks to be buried in the same cemetery. Yet even in death, Newt Knight was defiant. He left careful instructions for his funeral and was buried on a high ridge overlooking his old farmstead in a simple pine box beside Rachel, who had died in 1889. The inscription on his tombstone reads, "He Lived for Others."
By __James R. Kelly Jr.__ #11

 This is Newts second wife. She was a black slave that Newt rescued from the hands of her cruel master. Go to the theaters and see "The Free State of Jones" this is what it is about. It will certainly open your eyes to truth. Below you will find some of the scandal's in and around the Whitehouse.

Below is more information on the KKK Ku Klux Klan and heinous acts of torture! Done all in the name of the Democratic Party!

אֵל עוֹלָם

"Although it is relatively unreported today, historical documents are unequivocal that the Klan was established by Democrats and that the Klan played a prominent role in the Democratic Party," Barton writes in his book. "In fact, a 13-volume set of congressional investigations from 1872 conclusively and irrefutably documents that fact.

"Of all forms of violent intimidation, lynchings were by far the most effective," Barton said in his book. "Republicans often led the efforts to pass federal anti-lynching laws and their platforms consistently called for a ban on lynching. Democrats successfully blocked those bills and their platforms never did condemn lynchings."

*Further, the first grand wizard of the KKK was honored at the **1868 Democratic National Convention**, no Democrats voted for the 14th Amendment to grant citizenship to former slaves and, to this day, the party website ignores those decades of racism, he said.*

David Barton/Wallbuilders *#12*

19

"The Klan terrorized black Americans through murders and public floggings; relief was granted only if individuals promised not to vote for Republican tickets, and violation of this oath was punishable by death," he said. "Since the Klan targeted Republicans in general, it did not limit its violence simply to black Republicans; white Republicans were also included."
by (IrishMike 2009) #13

Fact: The Republican Party was founded primarily to oppose slavery, and Republicans eventually abolished slavery. The Democratic Party fought them and tried to maintain and expand slavery. The 13th Amendment, abolishing slavery, passed in 1865 with 100% Republican support but only 23% Democrat support in congress.
(2011 RussP.us) #14

אֵל עוֹלָם

By April 1865 the Confederate rebellion had been crushed and the American Civil War was finally over. Mississippi was occupied by Federal troops sent to maintain order and to protect the civil rights of former slaves. Captain Newt Knight was called into service by the United States Army as a commissioner in charge of distributing thousands of pounds of food to the poor and starving people in the Jones County area. Newt was also sent to rescue several black children who were still being held in slavery in Smith County.

So many blacks have no concept of this! They just listen to the media of today that squelch the truth! The truth is NOT being taught in the public school systems today. United States of America is a federal republic composed of 50 states. This is the pledge that we Americans came up with to represent how we stand as a nation. **"I pledge allegiance to the flag of the United States of America, and to the REPUBLIC for which it stands. One nation, under GOD. Indivisible. With liberty and justice for all."**
Notice it states to the REPUBLIC not a democracy.

Separation of Church and State Debunked

A conservative is a person tending to be moderate or cautious favoring the preservation of established customs, values. I'm sorry to burst anyone's bubble but this world does not belong to us, it is Gods! The bible tells us that God does NOT change He is the same yesterday, today and forever. Now wouldn't it stand to reason that He expects no less of us? Hence a conservative is only obeying what the creator wanted and still wants! To accept His 10 Commandments and to obey them would be one of His prerequisites.

A liberal on the other hand is a person favoring reform, open to new ideas, and tolerant of the ideas and behavior of others; not bound by traditional thinking. This I'm sorry folks, is counter to what creator God wants. This is free thinking and thinking that is against what God wants from us as His created beings. They want to reject the moral law of God and make up their own laws to fit their sin.

It comes right back again to good vs evil and they will always disagree because it is contrary (In hostile opposition or resistance to) to one another. Please forgive me but which side do you really choose to be on?

The right to keep religion in check is what the Founding Fathers placed in the section dedicated to not having the government control religion. That people would be free to worship the way they believed they should. The Founding Fathers knew if they didn't enact this it would be as it was before they ever came to America. Today the government and many people take this out of context to mean something different.

אֵל עוֹלָם

David Barton Quote: Thomas Jefferson had no intention of allowing the government to limit, restrict, regulate, or interfere with public religious practices. He believed, along with the other Founders, that the First Amendment had been enacted only to prevent the federal establishment of a national denomination – a fact he made clear in a letter to fellow-signer of the Declaration of Independence Benjamin Rush:

[T]he clause of the Constitution which, while it secured the freedom of the press, covered also the freedom of religion, had given to the clergy a very favorite hope of obtaining an establishment of a particular form of Christianity through the United States; and as every sect believes its own from the true one, every one perhaps hoped for his own, but especially the Episcopalians and Congregationalists. The returning good sense of our country threatens abortion to their hopes and they believe that any portion of power confided to me will be exerted in opposition to their schemes. And they believe rightly.

Jefferson had committed himself as President to pursuing the purpose of the First Amendment: preventing the "establishment of a particular form of Christianity" by the Episcopalians, Congregationalists, or any other denomination.

Since this was Jefferson's view concerning religious expression, in his short and polite reply to the Danbury Baptists on January 1, 1802, he assured them that they need not fear; that the free exercise of religion would never be interfered with by the federal government. As he explained:

Jefferson believed that God, not government, was the Author and Source of our rights and that the government, therefore, was to be prevented from interference with those rights. Very simply, the "fence" of the Webster letter and the "wall" of the Danbury letter were not to limit religious activities in public; rather they were to limit the power of the government to prohibit or interfere with those expressions.

David Barton (Wall Builders) 2001   #15

Although most people believe the words "separation of church and state" are actually in the U.S. Constitution, the words cannot be found there. Rather, they are words penned by Thomas Jefferson in a letter which explains the First Amendment of the Constitution or at least Jefferson's view of it. The actual words in the First Amendment of the Constitution read as follows: **"Congress shall make no law respecting an establishment of religion, or prohibiting the free exercise thereof. . . ."**

"Wall of separation between church and state"—History of phrase
In the fall of 1801, the Danbury (Conn.) Baptist Association sent Jefferson a written address congratulating him on his election. In his reply on January 1, 1802, Jefferson penned these now famous words:

I contemplate with sovereign reverence that act of the whole American people which declared that their legislature should "make no law respecting an establishment of religion, or prohibiting the free exercise thereof," thus building a wall of separation between Church & State."
http://www.allabouthistory.org/separation-of-church-and-state-in-the-constitution-faq.htm   #16

This was a letter written to Danbury Baptist Association. There has never been in the Constitution anything pertaining to "The Wall of Separation" This was merely Jefferson wishes for the American people being expressed to the Danbury Baptist Association. What he was trying to get across was the message that no government shall interfere with the free expression of a person's religion, and that the government would never interfere with matters of the church.

Below is the constitution. In case you want to read it all, if not, I have highlighted the parts that are pertinent and you can scroll through to see them. The bill of rights is also included and again I have highlighted the pertinent parts. You will also find All of the Amendments, with same highlighted. You see I believe an educated person is well equipped to make better judgment concerning all matters. In the following pages you'll find the entire Constitution, Amendments, and the Bill of Rights.

As you read, please meditate on all of the content. Learn the truth and the facts that will help you to make an informed decision at the voting polls! If you are a Christian you must vote as the Bible tells us to. Vote the candidate that shows they are going to rule as close as they can to the Bible!   In the next page this will begin with the Constitution.

THE CONSTITUTION OF THE UNITED STATES OF AMERICA

As Amended

Unratified Amendments

Analytical Index

UNUM
E
PLURIBUS

PRESENTED BY MR. BRADY OF PENNSYLVANIA

July 25, 2007 • Ordered to be printed

UNITED STATES GOVERNMENT PRINTING OFFICE WASHINGTON: 2007

For sale by the Superintendent of Documents, U.S. Government Printing Office Internet: bookstore.gpo.gov

Phone: toll free (866) 512-1800; DC area (202) 512-1800 Fax: (202) 512-2104 Mail: Stop IDCC, Washington, DC 20402-001 [ISBN 978-0-16-079091-1]

VerDate Aug 31 2005 11:11 Dec 10, 2007 Jkt 036932 PO 00000 Frm 00001 Fmt 5229 Sfmt 5229 E:\HR\OC\36932.X

CONSTITUTION OF THE UNITED STATES

WE THE PEOPLE *of the United States, in Order to form a more perfect Union, establish Justice, insure domestic Tranquility, provide for the common defence, [defense] promote the general Welfare, and secure the Blessings of Liberty to ourselves and our Posterity, do ordain and establish this Constitution for the United States of America.*

ARTICLE I.

SECTION 1. *All legislative Powers herein granted shall be vested in a Congress of the United States, which shall consist of a Senate and House of Representatives.*

1 *This text of the Constitution follows the engrossed copy signed by Gen. Washington and the deputies from 12 States. The small superior figures preceding the paragraphs designate clauses, and were not in the original and have no reference to footnotes. The Constitution was adopted by a convention of the States on September 17, 1787, and was subsequently ratified by the several States, on the following dates: Delaware, December 7, 1787; **Pennsylvania,** December 12, 1787; **New Jersey**, December 18, 1787; **Georgia**, January 2, 1788; **Connecticut,** January 9, 1788; **Massachusetts,** February 6, 1788; **Maryland,** April 28, 1788; **South Carolina,** May 23, 1788; **New Hampshire,** June 21, 1788. Ratification was completed on June 21, 1788. The Constitution was subsequently ratified by **Virginia,** June 25, 1788; **New York,** July 26, 1788; **North Carolina,** November 21, 1789; **Rhode Island,** May 29, 1790; and **Vermont,** January 10, 1791. In May 1785, a committee of Congress made a report recommending an alteration in the Articles of Confederation, but no action was taken on it, and it was left to the State Legislatures to proceed in the matter. In January 1786, the Legislature of Virginia passed a resolution providing for the appointment of five commissioners, who, or any three of them, should meet such commissioners as might be appointed in the other States of the Union, at a time and place to be agreed upon, to take into consideration the trade of the United States; to consider how far a uniform system in their commercial regulations may be necessary to their common interest and their permanent harmony; and to report to the several States such an act, relative to this great object, as, when ratified by them, will enable the United States in Congress effectually to provide for the same. The Virginia commissioners, after some correspondence, fixed the first Monday in September as the time, and the city of Annapolis as the place for the meeting, but only four other States were represented, viz: Delaware, New York, New Jersey, and Pennsylvania; the commissioners appointed by Massachusetts, New Hampshire, North Carolina, and Rhode Island failed to attend.*

Under the circumstances of so partial a representation, the commissioners present agreed upon a report (drawn by Mr. Hamilton, of New York) expressing their unanimous conviction that it might essentially tend to advance the interests of the Union if the States by which they were respectively delegated would concur, and use their endeavors to procure the concurrence of the other States, in the appointment of commissioners to meet at Philadelphia on the second Monday of May following, to take into consideration the situation of the United States; to devise such further provisions as should appear to them necessary to render the Constitution of the Federal Government adequate to the exigencies of the Union; and to report such an act for that purpose to the

United States in Congress assembled as, when agreed to by them and afterwards confirmed by the Legislatures of every State, would effectually provide for the same. Congress, on the 21st of February, 1787, adopted a resolution in favor of a convention, and the Legislatures of those States which had not already done so (with the exception of Rhode Island) promptly appointed delegates. On the 25th of May, seven States having convened, George Washington, of Virginia, was unanimously elected President, and the consideration of the proposed constitution was commenced. On the 17th of September, 1787, the Constitution as engrossed and agreed upon was signed by all the members present, except Mr. Gerry of Massachusetts, and Messrs. Mason and Randolph, of Virginia. The president of the convention transmitted it to Congress, with a resolution stating how the proposed Federal Government should be put in operation, and an explanatory letter. Congress, on the 28th of September, 1787, directed the Constitution so framed, with the resolutions and letter concerning the same, to "be transmitted to the several Legislatures in order to be submitted to a convention of delegates chosen in each State by the people thereof, in conformity to the resolves of the convention." On the 4th of March, 1789, the day which had been fixed for commencing the operations of Government under the new Constitution, it had been ratified by the conventions chosen in each State to consider it, as follows: Delaware, December 7, 1787; Pennsylvania, December 12, 1787; New Jersey, December 18, 1787; Georgia, January 2, 1788; Connecticut, January 9, 1788; Massachusetts, February 6, 1788; Maryland, April 28, 1788; South Carolina, May 23, 1788; New Hampshire, June 21, 1788; Virginia, June 25, 1788; and New York, July 26, 1788. The President informed Congress, on the 28th of January, 1790, that North Carolina had ratified the Constitution November 21, 1789; and he informed Congress on the 1st of June, 1790, that Rhode Island had ratified the Constitution May 29, 1790. Vermont, in convention, ratified the Constitution January 10, 1791, and was, by an act of Congress approved February 18, 1791, "received and admitted into this Union as a new and entire member of the United States." 2The part of this clause relating to the mode of apportionment of representatives among the several States has been affected by section 2 of amendment XIV, and as to taxes on incomes without apportionment by amendment XVI. 3This clause has been affected by clause 1 of amendment XVII.

SECTION 2. *1 The House of Representatives shall be composed of Members chosen every second Year by the People of the several States, and the Electors in each State shall have the Qualifications requisite for Electors of the most numerous Branch of the State Legislature. 2 No Person shall be a Representative who shall not have attained to the Age of twenty five Years, and been seven Years a Citizen of the United States, and who shall not, when elected, be an Inhabitant of that State in which he shall be chosen. 3 Representatives and direct Taxes shall be apportioned among the several States which may be included within this Union, according to their respective Numbers, which shall be determined by adding to the whole Number of free Persons, including those bound to Service for a Term of Years, and excluding Indians not taxed, three fifths of all other Persons.2 The actual Enumeration shall be made within three Years after the first Meeting of the Congress of the United States, and within every subsequent Term of ten Years, in such Manner as they shall by Law direct. The Number of Representatives shall not exceed one for every thirty Thousand, but each State shall have at Least one Representative; and until such enumeration shall be made, the State of New Hampshire*

shall be entitled to chuse three, Massachusetts eight, Rhode Island and Providence Plantations one, Connecticut five, New York six, New Jersey four, Pennsylvania eight, Delaware one, Maryland six, Virginia ten, North Carolina five, South Carolina five, and Georgia three. 4 When vacancies happen in the Representation from any State, the Executive Authority thereof shall issue Writs of Election to fill such Vacancies. 5 The House of Representatives shall chuse their Speaker and other Officers; and shall have the sole Power of Impeachment.

SECTION 3. *1 The Senate of the United States shall be composed of two Senators from each State, chosen by the Legislature thereof3 for six Years; and each Senator shall have one Vote. 2 Immediately after they shall be assembled in Consequence of the first Election, they shall be divided as equally as may be into three Classes. The Seats of the Senators of the first Class shall be vacated at the Expiration of the second Year, of the second Class at the Expiration of the fourth Year, and of the third Class at the Expiration of the sixth Year, so that one third may be chosen every*

VerDate Aug 31 2005 11:19 Dec 10, 2007 Jkt 036932 PO 00000 Frm 00008 Fmt 7601 Sfmt 7601 E:\HR\OC\932.CC 932

4 This clause has been affected by clause 2 of amendment XVIII. 5 This clause has been affected by amendment XX. second Year; and if Vacancies happen by Resignation or otherwise, during the Recess of the Legislature of any State, the Executive thereof may make temporary Appointments until the next Meeting of the Legislature, which shall then fill such Vacancies.4

3 No Person shall be a Senator who shall not have attained to the Age of thirty Years, and been nine Years a Citizen of the United States, and who shall not, when elected, be an Inhabitant of that State for which he shall be chosen. **4** The Vice President of the United States shall be President of the Senate, but shall have no Vote, unless they be equally divided. **5** The Senate shall chuse their other Officers, and also a President pro tempore, in the Absence of the Vice President, or when he shall exercise the Office of President of the United States. **6** The Senate shall have the sole Power to try all Impeachments. When sitting for that Purpose, they shall be on Oath or Affirmation. When the President of the United States is tried, the Chief Justice shall preside: And no Person shall be convicted without the Concurrence of two thirds of the Members present. **7** Judgment in Cases of Impeachment shall not extend further than to removal from Office, and disqualification to hold and enjoy any Office of honor, Trust or Profit under the United States: but the Party convicted shall nevertheless be liable and subject to Indictment, Trial, Judgment and Punishment, according to Law.

SECTION 4. **1** The Times, Places and Manner of holding Elections for Senators and Representatives, shall be prescribed in each State by the Legislature thereof; but the Congress may at any time by Law make or alter such Regulations, except as to the Places of chusing Senators. **2** The Congress shall assemble at least once in every Year and such Meeting shall be on the first Monday in December,5 unless they shall by Law appoint a different Day.

SECTION 5. **1** Each House shall be the Judge of the Elections, Returns and Qualifications of its own Members, and a Majority of each shall constitute a Quorum to do Business; but a smaller Number may adjourn from day to day, and may be authorized to compel the Attendance of absent Members, in such Manner, and under such Penalties as each House may provide. **2** Each House may determine the Rules of its Proceedings, punish its Members for disorderly Behavior, and, with the Concurrence of two thirds, expel a Member. **3** Each House shall keep a Journal of its Proceedings, and from time to time publish the same, excepting such Parts as may in their Judgment require Secrecy; and the Yeas and Nays of the Members of either House on any question shall, at the Desire of one fifth of those Present, be entered on the Journal. **4** Neither House, during the Session of Congress, shall, without the Consent of the other, adjourn for more than three days, nor to any other Place than that in which the two Houses shall be sitting.

SECTION 6. **1** The Senators and Representatives shall receive a Compensation for their Services, to be ascertained by Law, and paid out of the Treasury of the United States

VerDate Aug 31 2005 11:19 Dec 10, 2007 Jkt 036932 PO 00000 Frm 00009 Fmt 7601 Sfmt 7601 E:\HR\OC\932.CC 932 cprice-sewell on PROD1PC72 with HEARING

This clause has been affected by clause 2 of amendment XVIII.
This clause has been affected by amendment XX.

6 *They shall in all Cases, except Treason, Felony and Breach of the Peace, be privileged from Arrest during their Attendance at the Session of their respective Houses, and in going to and returning from the same; and for any Speech or Debate in either House, they shall not be questioned in any other Place.* **2** *No Senator or Representative shall, during the Time for which he was elected, be appointed to any civil Office under the Authority of the United States, which shall have been created, or the Emoluments whereof shall have been encreased [increased] during such time; and no Person holding any Office under the United States, shall be a Member of either House during his Continuance in Office.*

SECTION 7. 1 *All Bills for raising Revenue shall originate in the House of Representatives; but the Senate may propose or concur with Amendments as on other Bills.* **2** *Every Bill which shall have passed the House of Representatives and the Senate, shall, before it become a Law, be presented to the President of the United States; If he approve he shall sign it, but if not he shall return it, with his Objections to that House in which it shall have originated, who shall enter the Objections at large on their Journal, and proceed to reconsider it. If after such Reconsideration two thirds of that House shall agree to pass the Bill, it shall be sent, together with the Objections, to the other House, by which it shall likewise be reconsidered, and if approved by two thirds of that House, it shall become a Law. But in all such Cases the Votes of both Houses shall be determined by Yeas and Nays, and the Names of the Persons voting for and against the Bill shall be entered on the Journal of each House respectively. If any Bill shall not be returned by the President within ten Days (Sundays excepted) after it shall have been presented to him, the same shall be a Law, in like Manner as if he had signed it, unless the Congress by their Adjournment prevent its Return, in which Case it shall not be a Law.* **3** *Every Order, Resolution, or Vote to which the Concurrence of the Senate and House of Representatives may be necessary (except on a question of Adjournment) shall be presented to the President of the United States; and before the Same shall take Effect, shall be approved by him, or being disapproved by him, shall be repassed by two thirds of the Senate and House of Representatives, according to the Rules and Limitations prescribed in the Case of a Bill.*

SECTION 8. 1*The Congress shall have Power To lay and collect Taxes, Duties, Imposts and Excises, to pay the Debts and provide for the common Defence and general Welfare of the United States; but all Duties, Imposts and Excises shall be uniform throughout the United States;* **2** *To borrow Money on the credit of the United States;* **3** *To regulate Commerce with foreign Nations, and among the several States, and with the Indian Tribes;* **4** *To establish a uniform Rule of Naturalization, and uniform Laws on the subject of Bankruptcies throughout the United States;* **5** *To coin Money, regulate the Value thereof, and of foreign Coin, and fix the Standard of Weights and Measures;*

VerDate Aug 31 2005 11:19 Dec 10, 2007 Jkt 036932 PO 00000 Frm 00010 Fmt 7601 Sfmt 7601 E:\HR\OC\932.CC 932

This clause has been affected by amendment XVI.

6 To provide for the Punishment of counterfeiting the Securities and current Coin of the United States; **7** To establish Post Offices and post Roads; **8** To promote the Progress of Science and useful Arts, by securing for limited Times to Authors and Inventors the exclusive Right to their respective Writings and Discoveries; **9** To constitute Tribunals inferior to the supreme Court; **10** To define and punish Piracies and Felonies committed on the high Seas, and Offences against the Law of Nations; **11** To declare War, grant Letters of Marque and Reprisal, and make Rules concerning Captures on Land and Water; **12** To raise and support Armies, but no Appropriation of Money to that Use shall be for a longer Term than two Years; **13** To provide and maintain a Navy; **14** To make Rules for the Government and Regulation of the land and naval Forces; **15** To provide for calling forth the Militia to execute the Laws of the Union, suppress Insurrections and repel Invasions; **16** To provide for organizing, arming, and disciplining, the Militia, and for governing such Part of them as may be employed in the Service of the United States, reserving to the States respectively, the Appointment of the Officers, and the Authority of training the Militia according to the discipline prescribed by Congress; **17** To exercise exclusive Legislation in all Cases whatsoever, over such District (not exceeding ten Miles square) as may, by Cession of particular States, and the Acceptance of Congress, become the Seat of the Government of the United States, and to exercise like Authority over all Places purchased by the Consent of the Legislature of the State in which the Same shall be, for the Erection of Forts, Magazines, Arsenals, dock-Yards, and other needful buildings;—And **18** To make all Laws which shall be necessary and proper for carrying into Execution the foregoing Powers, and all other Powers vested by this Constitution in the Government of the United States, or in any Department or Officer thereof.

SECTION 9. 1 The Migration or Importation of such Persons as any of the States now existing shall think proper to admit, shall not be prohibited by the Congress prior to the Year one thousand eight hundred and eight, but a Tax or duty may be imposed on such Importation, not exceeding ten dollars for each Person. **2** The Privilege of the Writ of Habeas Corpus shall not be suspended, unless when in Cases of Rebellion or Invasion the public Safety may require it. **3** No Bill of Attainder or ex post facto Law shall be passed. **4** No Capitation, or other direct, Tax shall be laid, unless in Proportion to the Census or Enumeration herein before directed to be taken. **5** No Tax or Duty shall be laid on Articles exported from any State. **6** No Preference shall be given by any Regulation of Commerce or Revenue to the Ports of one State over those of another: nor shall

VerDate Aug 31 2005 11:19 Dec 10, 2007 Jkt 036932 PO 00000 Frm 00011 Fmt 7601 Sfmt 7601 E:\HR\OC\932.CC
932 cprice-sewell on PROD1PC72 with HEARING

Vessels bound to, or from, one State, be obliged to enter, clear, or pay Duties in another. **7** No Money shall be drawn from the Treasury, but in Consequence of Appropriations made by Law; and a regular Statement and Account of the Receipts and Expenditures of all public Money shall be published from time to time. **8** No Title of Nobility shall be granted by the United States: And no Person holding any Office of Profit or Trust under them, shall, without the Consent of the Congress, accept of any present, Emolument, Office, or Title, of any kind whatever, from any King, Prince, or foreign State.

SECTION 10. 1 No State shall enter into any Treaty, Alliance, or Confederation; grant Letters of Marque and Reprisal; coin Money; emit Bills of Credit; make any Thing but gold and silver Coin a Tender in Payment of Debts; pass any Bill of Attainder, ex post facto Law, or Law impairing the Obligation of Contracts, or grant any Title of Nobility. **2** No State shall, without the Consent of the Congress, lay any Imposts or Duties on Imports or Exports, except what may be absolutely necessary for executing its inspection Laws: and the net Produce of all Duties and Imposts, laid by any State on Imports or Exports, shall be for the Use of the Treasury of the United States; and all such Laws shall be subject to the Revision and Control of the Congress. **3** No State shall, without the Consent of Congress, lay any Duty of Tonnage, keep Troops, or Ships of War in time of Peace, enter into any Agreement or Compact with another State, or with a foreign Power, or engage in War, unless actually invaded, or in such imminent Danger as will not admit of delay.

ARTICLE II.

SECTION 1. 1The executive Power shall be vested in a President of the United States of America. He shall hold his Office during the Term of four Years, and, together with the Vice President, chosen for the same Term, be elected, as follows **2** Each State shall appoint, in such Manner as the Legislature thereof may direct, a Number of Electors, equal to the whole Number of Senators and Representatives to which the State may be entitled in the Congress: but no Senator or Representative, or Person holding an Office of Trust or Profit under the United States, shall be appointed an Elector. **3** The Electors shall meet in their respective States, and vote by Ballot for two Persons, of whom one at least shall not be an Inhabitant of the same State with themselves. And they shall make a List of all the Persons voted for, and of the Number of Votes for each; which List they shall sign and certify, and transmit sealed to the Seat of the Government of the United States, directed to the President of the Senate.

The President of the Senate shall, in the Presence of the Senate and House of Representatives, open all the Certificates, and the Votes shall then be counted. The Person having the greatest Number of Votes shall be the President, if such Number be a Majority of the whole Number of Electors appointed; and if there be more than one who have such Majority, and have an equal Number of Votes, then the House of Representatives shall

VerDate Aug 31 2005 11:19 Dec 10, 2007 Jkt 036932 PO 00000 Frm 00012 Fmt 7601 Sfmt 7601 E:\HR\OC\932.CC 932 cprice-sewell on PROD1PC72 with HEARING

This clause has been superseded by amendment XII.
This clause has been affected by amendment XXV.

immediately chuse by Ballot one of them for President;8 and if no Person have a Majority, then from the five highest on the List the said House shall in like Manner chuse the President. But in chusing the President, the Votes shall be taken by States, the Representation from each State having one Vote; A quorum for this Purpose shall consist of a Member or Members from two thirds of the States, and a Majority of all the States shall be necessary to a Choice. In every Case, after the Choice of the President, the Person having the greatest Number of Votes of the Electors shall be the Vice President. But if there should remain two or more who have equal Votes, the Senate shall chuse from them by Ballot the Vice President.8 4The Congress may determine the Time of chusing the Electors, and the Day on which they shall give their Votes; which Day shall be the same throughout the United States. 5No Person except a natural born Citizen, or a Citizen of the United States, at the time of the Adoption of this Constitution, shall be eligible to the Office of President; neither shall any Person be eligible to that Office who shall not have attained to the Age of thirty five Years, and been fourteen Years a Resident within the United States. 6In Case of the Removal of the President from Office, or of his Death, Resignation, or Inability to discharge the Powers and Duties of the said Office,9 the Same shall devolve on the Vice President, and the Congress may by Law provide for the Case of Removal, Death, Resignation or Inability, both of the President and Vice President, declaring what Officer shall then act as President, and such Officer shall act accordingly, until the Disability be removed, or a President shall be elected. 7The President shall, at stated Times, receive for his Services, a Compensation, which shall neither be encreased nor diminished during the Period for which he shall have been elected, and he shall not receive within that Period any other Emolument from the United States, or any of them. 8Before he enter on the Execution of his Office, he shall take the following Oath or Affirmation:—"I do solemnly swear (or affirm) that I will faithfully execute the Office of President of the United States, and will to the best of my Ability, preserve, protect and defend the Constitution of the United States."

SECTION 2.

1 The President shall be Commander in Chief of the Army and Navy of the United States, and of the Militia of the several States, when called into the actual Service of the United States; he may require the Opinion, in writing, of the principal Officer in each of the executive Departments, upon any Subject relating to the Duties of their respective Offices, and he shall have Power to grant Reprieves and Pardons for Offences against the United States, except in Cases of Impeachment. **2** He shall have Power, by and with the Advice and Consent of the Senate, to make Treaties, provided two thirds of the Senators present concur; and he shall nominate, and by and with the Advice and Consent of the Senate, shall appoint Ambassadors, other public Ministers and Consuls, Judges of the supreme Court, and all other Officers of the United States, whose

This clause has been affected by amendment XI.

Appointments are not herein otherwise provided for, and which shall be established by Law: but the Congress may by Law vest the Appointment of such inferior Officers, as they think proper, in the President alone, in the Courts of Law, or in the Heads of Departments. **3** The President shall have Power to fill up all Vacancies that may happen during the Recess of the Senate, by granting Commissions which shall expire at the End of their next Session.

SECTION 3. He shall from time to time give to the Congress Information of the State of the Union, and recommend to their Consideration such Measures as he shall judge necessary and expedient; he may, on extraordinary Occasions, convene both Houses, or either of them, and in Case of Disagreement between them, with Respect to the Time of Adjournment, he may adjourn them to such Time as he shall think proper; he shall receive Ambassadors and other public Ministers; he shall take Care that the Laws be faithfully executed, and shall Commission all the Officers of the United States. **SECTION 4**. *The President, Vice President and all civil Officers of the United States, shall be removed from Office on Impeachment for, and Conviction of, Treason, Bribery, or other high Crimes and Misdemeanors.*

ARTICLE III.

SECTION 1. The judicial Power of the United States, shall be vested in one supreme Court, and in such inferior Courts as the Congress may from time to time ordain and establish. The Judges, both of the supreme and inferior Courts, shall hold their Offices during good Behaviour, and shall, at stated Times, receive for their Services, a Compensation, which shall not be diminished during their Continuance in Office.

SECTION 2. **1** The judicial Power shall extend to all Cases, in Law and Equity, arising under this Constitution, the Laws of the United States, and Treaties made, or which shall be made, under their Authority;—to all Cases affecting Ambassadors, other public Ministers and Consuls;—to all Cases of admiralty and maritime Jurisdiction;—to

Controversies to which the United States will be a party;—to Controversies between two or more States;—between a State and Citizens of another State;10—between Citizens of different States,—between Citizens of the same State claiming Lands under Grants of different States, and between a State, or the Citizens thereof, and foreign States, Citizens or Subjects. *2* In all Cases affecting Ambassadors, other public Ministers and Consuls, and those in which a State shall be Party, the supreme Court shall have original Jurisdiction. In all the other Cases before mentioned, the supreme Court shall have appellate Jurisdiction, both as to Law and Fact, with such Exceptions, and under such Regulations as the Congress shall make. *3* The Trial of all Crimes, except in Cases of Impeachment, shall be by Jury; and such Trial shall be held in the State where the said Crimes shall have been committed; but when not committed within any State, the Trial shall be at such Place or Places as the Congress may by Law have directed.

SECTION 3.

1 Treason against the United States, shall consist only in levying War against them, or in <u>adhering</u> to their Enemies, giving them Aid and Comfort. No Person shall be convicted of Treason unless on the Testimony of two Witnesses to the same overt Act, or on Confession in open Court.

The Congress shall have Power to declare the Punishment of Treason, but no Attainder of Treason shall work Corruption of Blood, or Forfeiture except during the Life of the Person attainted.

ARTICLE IV.

SECTION 1. Full Faith and Credit shall be given in each State to the public Acts, Records, and judicial Proceedings of every other State. And the Congress may by general Laws prescribe the Manner in which such Acts, Records and Proceedings shall be proved, and the Effect thereof.

SECTION 2. 1 The Citizens of each State shall be entitled to all Privileges and Immunities of Citizens in the several States. *2* A Person charged in any State with Treason, Felony, or other Crime, who shall flee from Justice, and be found in another State, shall on Demand of the executive Authority of the State from which he fled, be delivered up, to be removed to the State having Jurisdiction of the Crime. *3* No Person held to Service or Labour in one State, under the Laws thereof, escaping into another, shall, in Consequence of any Law or Regulation therein, be discharged from such Service or Labour, but shall be delivered up on Claim of the Party to whom such Service or Labour may be due.11

SECTION 3. 1 New States may be admitted by the Congress into this Union; but no new State shall be formed or erected within the Jurisdiction of any other State; nor any State be formed by the Junction of two or more States, or Parts of States, without the Consent of the Legislatures of the States concerned as well as of the Congress. *2* The Congress shall have Power to dispose of and make all needful Rules and Regulations respecting the Territory or other Property belonging to the United States; and nothing in this

Constitution shall be so construed as to Prejudice any Claims of the United States, or of any particular State.

SECTION 4. *The United States shall guarantee to every State in this Union a Republican Form of Government, and shall protect each of them against Invasion; and on Application of the Legislature, or of the Executive (when the Legislature cannot be convened) against domestic Violence.*

ARTICLE V.

The Congress, whenever two thirds of both Houses shall deem it necessary, shall propose Amendments to this Constitution, or, on the Application of the Legislatures of two thirds of the several States, shall call a Convention for proposing Amendments, which, in either Case, shall be valid to all Intents and Purposes, as Part of this Constitution, when ratified by the Legislatures of three fourths of the several States, or by Conventions in three fourths thereof, as the one or the other Mode of Ratification may be proposed by the Congress; Provided that no Amendment which may be made prior to the Year One thousand eight hundred and eight shall in any Manner affect the first and fourth Clauses in the Ninth Section of the first Article; and that no State, without its Consent, shall be deprived of its equal Suffrage in the Senate.

This clause has been affected by amendment XIII.

ARTICLE VI.

1 All Debts contracted and Engagements entered into, before the Adoption of this Constitution, shall be as valid against the United States under this Constitution, as under the Confederation. 2 This Constitution, and the Laws of the United States which shall be made in Pursuance thereof; and all Treaties made, or which shall be made, under the Authority of the United States, shall be the supreme Law of the Land; and the Judges in every State shall be bound thereby, any Thing in the Constitution or Laws of any State to the Contrary notwithstanding. 3 The Senators and Representatives before mentioned, and the Members of the several State Legislatures, and all executive and judicial Officers, both of the United States and of the several States, shall be bound by Oath or Affirmation, to support this Constitution; but no religious Test shall ever be required as a Qualification to any Office or public Trust under the United States.

ARTICLE VII.

The Ratification of the Conventions of nine States, shall be sufficient for the Establishment of this Constitution between the States so ratifying the Same. DONE in Convention by the Unanimous Consent of the States present the Seventeenth Day of September in the Year of our Lord one thousand seven hundred and Eighty seven and of the Independence of the United States of America the Twelfth IN WITNESS whereof We have hereunto subscribed our Names, GO. WASHINGTON—Presidt. and deputy from Virginia.

CONSTITUTION OF THE UNITED STATES [Signed also by the deputies of twelve States.]

Delaware

GEO: READ

GUNNING BEDFORD

JOHN DICKINSON

RICHARD BASSETT

JACO: BROOM

Maryland

JAMES MCHENRY

DAN OF ST THOS JENIFER

DANL CARROLL

New Hampshire

JOHN LANGDON

NICHOLAS GILMAN

Massachusetts

NATHANIEL GORHAM

RUFUS KING

Connecticut

W M. SAML. JOHNSON

ROGER SHERMAN

Virginia

JOHN BLAIR

JAMES MADISON JR.

New York

ALEXANDER HAMILTON

North Carolina

WM BLOUNT

RICH D. DOBBS SPAIGHT

HU WILLIAMSON

New Jersey

W IL: LIVINGSTON

D AVID BREARLEY

W M. PATERSON

JONA: DAYTON

South Carolina	*Pennsylvania*
J. RUTLEDGE	B FRANKLIN
CHARLES COTESWORTH PINCKNEY	THOMAS MIFFLIN
CHARLES PINCKNEY	ROB т MORRIS
PIERCE BUTLER	GEO. CLYMER
	THOS. FITZSIMONS
Georgia	JARED INGERSOLL
WILLIAM FEW	JAMES WILSON
ABR BALDWIN	GOUV MORRIS

Attest: WILLIAM JACKSON Secretary

http://www.archives.gov/exhibits/charters/constitution_transcript.html

The Declaration of Independence: A Transcription

IN CONGRESS, July 4, 1776.

The unanimous Declaration of the thirteen united States of America,

When in the Course of human events, it becomes necessary for one people to dissolve the political bands which have connected them with another, and to assume among the powers of the earth, the separate and equal station to which the Laws of Nature and of Nature's God entitle them, a decent respect to the opinions of mankind requires that they should declare the causes which impel them to the separation.

We hold these truths to be self-evident, that all men are created equal, that they are endowed by their Creator with certain unalienable Rights, that among these are Life, Liberty and the pursuit of Happiness.--That to secure these rights, Governments are instituted among Men, deriving their just powers from the consent of the governed, -- **That whenever any Form of Government becomes destructive of these ends, it is the Right of the People to alter or to abolish it, and to institute new Government, laying its foundation on such principles and organizing its powers in such form, as to them shall seem most likely to effect [affect] their Safety and Happiness.** Prudence, indeed, will dictate that Governments long established should not be changed for light and transient causes; and accordingly all experience hath shewn,[shown] that mankind are more disposed to suffer, while evils are sufferable, than to right themselves by abolishing the forms to which they are accustomed. But when a long train of abuses and usurpations, pursuing invariably the same Object evinces a design to reduce them under absolute Despotism, it is their right, it is their duty, to throw off such Government, and to provide new Guards for their future security.--Such has been the patient sufferance of these Colonies; and such is now the necessity which constrains them to alter their former Systems of Government. The history of the present King of Great Britain is a history of repeated injuries and usurpations, all having in direct object the establishment of an absolute Tyranny over these States. To prove this, let Facts be submitted to a candid world.

He has refused his Assent to Laws, the most wholesome and necessary for the public good. He has forbidden his Governors to pass Laws of immediate and pressing importance, unless suspended in their operation till his Assent should be obtained; and when so suspended, he has utterly neglected to attend to them.

He has refused to pass other Laws for the accommodation of large districts of people, unless those people would relinquish the right of Representation in the Legislature, a right inestimable to them and formidable to tyrants only.

He has called together legislative bodies at places unusual, uncomfortable, and distant from the depository of their public Records, for the sole purpose of fatiguing them into compliance with his measures.

He has dissolved Representative Houses repeatedly, for opposing with manly firmness his invasions on the rights of the people.

He has refused for a long time, after such dissolutions, to cause others to be elected; whereby the Legislative powers, incapable of Annihilation, have returned to the People at large for their exercise; the State remaining in the meantime exposed to all the dangers of invasion from without, and convulsions within.

He has endeavored to prevent the population of these States; for that purpose obstructing the Laws for Naturalization of Foreigners; refusing to pass others to encourage their migrations hither, and raising the conditions of new Appropriations of Lands.

He has obstructed the Administration of Justice, by refusing his Assent to Laws for establishing Judiciary powers.

He has made Judges dependent on his Will alone, for the tenure of their offices, and the amount and payment of their salaries.

He has erected a multitude of New Offices, and sent hither swarms of Officers to harrass our people, and eat out their substance.

He has kept among us, in times of peace, Standing Armies without the Consent of our legislatures.

He has affected to render the Military independent of and superior to the Civil power.

He has combined with others to subject us to a jurisdiction foreign to our constitution, and unacknowledged by our laws; giving his Assent to their Acts of pretended Legislation:

For Quartering large bodies of armed troops among us:

For protecting them, by a mock Trial, from punishment for any Murders which they should commit on the Inhabitants of these States:

For cutting off our Trade with all parts of the world:

For imposing Taxes on us without our Consent:

For depriving us in many cases, of the benefits of Trial by Jury:

For transporting us beyond Seas to be tried for pretended offences

For abolishing the free System of English Laws in a neighboring Province, establishing therein an Arbitrary government, and enlarging its Boundaries so as to render it at once an example and fit instrument for introducing the same absolute rule into these Colonies:

For taking away our Charters, abolishing our most valuable Laws, and altering fundamentally the Forms of our Governments:

For suspending our own Legislatures, and declaring themselves invested with power to legislate for us in all cases whatsoever.

He has abdicated Government here, by declaring us out of his Protection and waging War against us.

He has plundered our seas, ravaged our Coasts, burnt our towns, and destroyed the lives of our people.

He is at this time transporting large Armies of foreign Mercenaries to compleat the works of death, desolation and tyranny, already begun with circumstances of Cruelty & perfidy scarcely paralleled in the most barbarous ages, and totally unworthy the Head of a civilized nation.

He has constrained our fellow Citizens taken Captive on the high Seas to bear Arms against their Country, to become the executioners of their friends and Brethren, or to fall themselves by their Hands.

He has excited domestic insurrections amongst us, and has endeavored to bring on the inhabitants of our frontiers, the merciless Indian Savages, whose known rule of warfare is an undistinguished destruction of all ages, sexes and conditions.

In every stage of these Oppressions We have petitioned for Redress in the most humble terms: Our repeated Petitions have been answered only by repeated injury. A Prince, whose character is thus marked by every act which may define a Tyrant, is unfit to be the ruler of a free people.

Nor have we been wanting in attentions to our Brittish brethren. We have warned them from time to time of attempts by their legislature to extend an unwarrantable jurisdiction over us. We have reminded them of the circumstances of our emigration and settlement here. We have appealed to their native justice and magnanimity, and we have conjured them by the ties of our common kindred to disavow these usurpations, which would inevitably interrupt our connections and correspondence. They too have been deaf to the voice of justice and of consanguinity. We must, therefore, acquiesce in the necessity, which denounces our Separation, and hold them, as we hold the rest of mankind, Enemies in War, in Peace Friends.

We, therefore, the Representatives of the united States of America, in General Congress, Assembled, appealing to the Supreme Judge of the world for the rectitude of our intentions, do, in the Name, and by Authority of the good People of these Colonies, solemnly publish and declare, That these United Colonies are, and of Right ought to be Free and Independent States; that they are Absolved from all Allegiance to the British Crown, and that all political connection between them and the State of Great

Britain, is and ought to be totally dissolved; and that as Free and Independent States, they have full Power to levy War, conclude Peace, contract Alliances, establish Commerce, and to do all other Acts and Things which Independent States may of right do. And for the support of this Declaration, with a firm reliance on the protection of divine Providence, we mutually pledge to each other our Lives, our Fortunes and our sacred Honor.

The 56 signatures on the Declaration appear in the positions indicated:

Column 1
Georgia:
   Button Gwinnett
   Lyman Hall
   George Walton

Column 2
North Carolina:
   William Hooper
   Joseph Hewes
   John Penn
South Carolina:
   Edward Rutledge
   Thomas Heyward, Jr.
   Thomas Lynch, Jr.
   Arthur Middleton

Column 3
Massachusetts:
John Hancock
Maryland:
Samuel Chase
William Paca
Thomas Stone
Charles Carroll of Carrollton
Virginia:
George Wythe
Richard Henry Lee
Thomas Jefferson
Benjamin Harrison
Thomas Nelson, Jr.
Francis Lightfoot Lee
Carter Braxton

Column 4
Pennsylvania:
   Robert Morris
   Benjamin Rush
   Benjamin Franklin
   John Morton
   George Clymer
   James Smith
   George Taylor
   James Wilson
   George Ross

Delaware:
  Caesar Rodney
  George Read
  Thomas McKean

Column 5
New York:
  William Floyd
  Philip Livingston
  Francis Lewis
  Lewis Morris
New Jersey:
  Richard Stockton
  John Witherspoon
  Francis Hopkinson
  John Hart
  Abraham Clark

Column 6
New Hampshire:
  Josiah Bartlett
  William Whipple
Massachusetts:
  Samuel Adams
  John Adams
  Robert Treat Paine
  Elbridge Gerry
Rhode Island:
  Stephen Hopkins
  William Ellery
Connecticut:
  Roger Sherman
  Samuel Huntington
  William Williams
  Oliver Wolcott
New Hampshire:
  Matthew Thornton

(http://www.archives.gov/exhibits/charters/constitution.html)

41

All Amendments to the United States Constitution

Amendments 1-10 | Amendments 11-27

Congress of the United States
begun and held at the City of New-York, on
Wednesday the fourth of March, one thousand seven hundred and eighty nine.

THE Conventions of a number of the States, having at the time of their adopting the Constitution, expressed a desire, in order to prevent misconstruction or abuse of its powers, that further declaratory and restrictive clauses should be added: And as extending the ground of public confidence in the Government, will best ensure the beneficent ends of its institution.

RESOLVED by the Senate and House of Representatives of the United States of America, in Congress assembled, two thirds of both Houses concurring, that the following Articles be proposed to the Legislatures of the several States, as amendments to the Constitution of the United States, all, or any of which Articles, when ratified by three fourths of the said Legislatures, to be valid to all intents and purposes, as part of the said Constitution; viz.

ARTICLES in addition to, and Amendment of the Constitution of the United States of America, proposed by Congress, and ratified by the Legislatures of the several States, pursuant to the fifth Article of the original Constitution.   *Note: The following text is a transcription of the first ten amendments to the Constitution in their original form. These amendments were ratified December 15, 1791, and form what is known as the "Bill of Rights."*

AMENDMENT I

Congress shall make no law respecting an establishment of religion, or prohibiting the free exercise thereof; or abridging the freedom of speech, or of the press; or the right of the people peaceably to assemble, and to petition the Government for a redress of grievances.

AMENDMENT II

A well regulated Militia, being necessary to the security of a free State, the right of the people to keep and bear Arms, shall not be infringed.

AMENDMENT III
No Soldier shall, in time of peace be quartered in any house, without the consent of the Owner, nor in time of war, but in a manner to be prescribed by law.

AMENDMENT II

The right of the people to be secure in their persons, houses, papers, and effects, against unreasonable searches and seizures, shall not be violated, and no Warrants shall issue, but upon probable cause, supported by Oath or affirmation, and particularly describing the place to be searched, and the persons or things to be seized.

AMENDMENT VII

No person shall be held to answer for a capital, or otherwise infamous crime, unless on a presentment or indictment of a Grand Jury, except in cases arising in the land or naval forces, or in the Militia, when in actual service in time of War or public danger; nor shall any person be subject for the same offence to be twice put in jeopardy of life or limb; nor shall be compelled in any criminal case to be a witness against himself, nor be deprived of life, liberty, or property, without due process of law; nor shall private property be taken for public use, without just compensation.

AMENDMENT VI

In all criminal prosecutions, the accused shall enjoy the right to a speedy and public trial, by an impartial jury of the State and district wherein the crime shall have been committed, which district shall have been previously ascertained by law, and to be informed of the nature and cause of the accusation; to be confronted with the witnesses against him; to have compulsory process for obtaining witnesses in his favor, and to have the Assistance of Counsel for his defence.

AMENDMENT VII

In Suits at common law, where the value in controversy shall exceed twenty dollars, the right of trial by jury shall be preserved, and no fact tried by a jury, shall be otherwise re-examined in any Court of the United States, than according to the rules of the common law.

AMENDMENT VIII

Excessive bail shall not be required, nor excessive fines imposed, nor cruel and unusual punishments inflicted.

AMENDMENT IX

The enumeration in the Constitution, of certain rights, shall not be construed to deny or disparage others retained by the people.

AMENDMENT X

The powers not delegated to the United States by the Constitution, nor prohibited by it to the States, are reserved to the States respectively, or to the people.

AMENDMENT XI - Passed by Congress March 4, 1794. Ratified February 7, 1795.

Note: Article III, section 2, of the Constitution was modified by amendment 11.

The Judicial power of the United States shall not be construed to extend to any suit in law or equity, commenced or prosecuted against one of the United States by Citizens of another State, or by Citizens or Subjects of any Foreign State.

AMENDMENT XII - Passed by Congress December 9, 1803. Ratified June 15, 1804.

Note: A portion of Article II, section 1 of the Constitution was superseded by the 12th amendment.

The Electors shall meet in their respective states and vote by ballot for President and Vice-President, one of whom, at least, shall not be an inhabitant of the same state with themselves; they shall name in their ballots the person voted for as President, and in distinct ballots the person voted for as Vice-President, and they shall make distinct lists of all persons voted for as President, and of all persons voted for as Vice-President, and of the number of votes for each, which lists they shall sign and certify, and transmit sealed to the seat of the government of the United States, directed to the President of the Senate; -- the President of the Senate shall, in the presence of the Senate and House of Representatives, open all the certificates and the votes shall then be counted; -- The person having the greatest number of votes for President, shall be the President, if such number be a majority of the whole number of Electors appointed; and if no person have such majority, then from the persons having the highest numbers not exceeding three on the list of those voted for as President, the House of Representatives shall choose immediately, by ballot, the President. But in choosing the President, the votes shall be taken by states, the representation from each state having one vote; a quorum for this purpose shall consist of a member or members from two-thirds of the states, and a majority of all the states shall be necessary to a choice. [And if the House of Representatives shall not choose a President whenever the right of choice shall devolve upon them, before the fourth day of March next following, then the Vice-President shall act as President, as in case of the death or other constitutional disability of the President. --]* The person having the greatest number of votes as Vice-President, shall be the Vice-President, if such number be a majority of the whole number of Electors appointed, and if no person have a majority, then from the two highest numbers on the list, the Senate shall choose the Vice-President; a quorum for the purpose shall consist of two-thirds of the whole number of Senators, and a majority of the whole number shall be necessary to a choice. But no person constitutionally ineligible to the office of President shall be eligible to that of Vice-President of the United States.   *Superseded by section 3 of the 20th amendment.*

AMENDMENT XIII - Passed by Congress January 31, 1865. Ratified December 6, 1865.*Note: A portion of Article IV, section 2, of the Constitution was superseded by the 13th amendment.*

Section 1.

Neither slavery nor involuntary servitude, except as a punishment for crime whereof the party shall have been duly convicted, shall exist within the United States, or any place subject to their jurisdiction.

Section 2.

Congress shall have power to enforce this article by appropriate legislation.

AMENDMENT XIV - Passed by Congress June 13, 1866. Ratified July 9, 1868. *Note: Article I, section 2, of the Constitution was modified by section 2 of the 14th amendment.*

Section 1.

All persons born or naturalized in the United States, and subject to the jurisdiction thereof, are citizens of the United States and of the State wherein they reside. No State shall make or enforce any law which shall abridge the privileges or immunities of citizens of the United States; nor shall any State deprive any person of life, liberty, or property, without due process of law; nor deny to any person within its jurisdiction the equal protection of the laws.

Section 2.

Representatives shall be apportioned among the several States according to their respective numbers, counting the whole number of persons in each State, excluding Indians not taxed. But when the right to vote at any election for the choice of electors for President and Vice-President of the United States, Representatives in Congress, **the Executive and Judicial officers of a State, or the members of the Legislature thereof, is denied to any of the male inhabitants of such State, being twenty-one years of age,* and citizens of the United States,** or in any way abridged, except for participation in rebellion, or other crime, the basis of representation therein shall be reduced in the proportion which the number of such male citizens shall bear to the whole number of male citizens twenty-one years of age in such State.

Section 3.

No person shall be a Senator or Representative in Congress, or elector of President and Vice-President, or hold any office, civil or military, under the United States, or under any State, who, having previously taken an oath, as a member of Congress, or as an officer of the United States, or as a member of any State legislature, or as an executive or judicial officer of any State, to support the Constitution of the United States, shall have engaged in insurrection or rebellion against the same, or given aid or comfort to the enemies thereof. But Congress may by a vote of two-thirds of each House, remove such disability.

Section 4.

The validity of the public debt of the United States, authorized by law, including debts incurred for payment of pensions and bounties for services in suppressing insurrection or rebellion, shall not be questioned. But neither the United States nor any State shall assume or pay any debt or obligation incurred in aid of insurrection or rebellion against the United States, or any claim for the loss or emancipation of any slave; but all such debts, obligations and claims shall be held illegal and void.

Section 5.
The Congress shall have the power to enforce, by appropriate legislation, the provisions of this article.

Changed by section 1 of the 26th amendment.

AMENDMENT XV - Passed by Congress February 26, 1869. Ratified February 3, 1870.

Section 1.
The right of citizens of the United States to vote shall not be denied or abridged by the United States or by any State on account of race, color, or previous condition of servitude--

Section 2.
The Congress shall have the power to enforce this article by appropriate legislation.

AMENDMENT XVI - Passed by Congress July 2, 1909. Ratified February 3, 1913.

Note: Article I, section 9, of the Constitution was modified by amendment 16.

The Congress shall have power to lay and collect taxes on incomes, from whatever source derived, without apportionment among the several States, and without regard to any census or enumeration.

AMENDMENT XVII - Passed by Congress May 13, 1912. Ratified April 8, 1913.

Note: Article I, section 3, of the Constitution was modified by the 17th amendment.

The Senate of the United States shall be composed of two Senators from each State, elected by the people thereof, for six years; and each Senator shall have one vote. The electors in each State shall have the qualifications requisite for electors of the most numerous branch of the State legislatures.

When vacancies happen in the representation of any State in the Senate, the executive authority of such State shall issue writs of election to fill such vacancies: Provided, that the legislature of any State may empower the executive thereof to make temporary appointments until the people fill the vacancies by election as the legislature may direct.

This amendment shall not be so construed as to affect the election or term of any Senator chosen before it becomes valid as part of the Constitution.

AMENDMENT XVIII - Passed by Congress December 18, 1917. Ratified January 16, 1919. Repealed by amendment 21.

Section 1.
After one year from the ratification of this article the manufacture, sale, or

transportation of intoxicating liquors within, the importation thereof into, or the exportation thereof from the United States and all territory subject to the jurisdiction thereof for beverage purposes is hereby prohibited.

Section 2.
The Congress and the several States shall have concurrent power to enforce this article by appropriate legislation.

Section 3.
This article shall be inoperative unless it shall have been ratified as an amendment to the Constitution by the legislatures of the several States, as provided in the Constitution, within seven years from the date of the submission hereof to the States by the Congress.

AMENDMENT XIX - Passed by Congress June 4, 1919. Ratified August 18, 1920.

The right of citizens of the United States to vote shall not be denied or abridged by the United States or by any State on account of sex.

Congress shall have power to enforce this article by appropriate legislation.

AMENDMENT XX – Passed by Congress March 2, 1932. Ratified January 23, 1933.

Note: Article I, section 4, of the Constitution was modified by section 2 of this amendment. In addition, a portion of the 12th amendment was superseded by section 3.

Section 1.
The terms of the President and the Vice President shall end at noon on the 20th day of January, and the terms of Senators and Representatives at noon on the 3 day of January, of the years in which such terms would have ended if this article had not been ratified; and the terms of their successors shall then begin.

Section 2.
The Congress shall assemble at least once in every year, and such meeting shall begin at noon on the 3d day of January, unless they shall by law appoint a different day.

Section 3.
If, at the time fixed for the beginning of the term of the President, the President elect shall have died, the Vice President elect shall become President.

If a President shall not have been chosen before the time fixed for the beginning of his term, or if the President elect shall have failed to qualify, then the Vice President elect shall act as President until a President shall have qualified; and the Congress may by law provide for the case wherein neither a President elect nor a Vice President shall have qualified, declaring who shall then act as President, or the manner in which one who is to act shall be selected, and such person shall act accordingly until a President or Vice President shall have qualified.

Section 4.
The Congress may by law provide for the case of the death of any of the persons from whom the House of Representatives may choose a President whenever the right of

choice shall have devolved upon them, and for the case of the death of any of the persons from whom the Senate may choose a Vice President whenever the right of choice shall have devolved upon them.

Section 5.
Sections 1 and 2 shall take effect on the 15th day of October following the ratification of this article.

Section 6.
This article shall be inoperative unless it shall have been ratified as an amendment to the Constitution by the legislatures of three-fourths of the several States within seven years from the date of its submission.

AMENDMENT XXI –Passed by Congress February 20, 1933. Ratified December 5, 1933.

Section 1.
The eighteenth article of amendment to the Constitution of the United States is hereby repealed.

Section 2.
The transportation or importation into any State, Territory, or Possession of the United States for delivery or use therein of intoxicating liquors, in violation of the laws thereof, is hereby prohibited.

Section 3.
This article shall be inoperative unless it shall have been ratified as an amendment to the Constitution by conventions in the several States, as provided in the Constitution, within seven years from the date of the submission hereof to the States by the Congress.

AMENDMENT XXII –Passed by Congress March 21, 1947. Ratified February 27, 1951.

Section 1.
No person shall be elected to the office of the President more than twice, and no person who has held the office of President, or acted as President, for more than two years of a term to which some other person was elected President shall be elected to the office of President more than once. But this Article shall not apply to any person holding the office of President when this Article was proposed by Congress, and shall not prevent any person who may be holding the office of President, or acting as President, during the term within which this Article becomes operative from holding the office of President or acting as President during the remainder of such term.

Section 2.
This article shall be inoperative unless it shall have been ratified as an amendment to the Constitution by the legislatures of three-fourths of the several States within seven years from the date of its submission to the States by the Congress.

AMENDMENT XXIII – Passed by Congress June 16, 1960. Ratified March 29, 1961.

Section 1.
The District constituting the seat of Government of the United States shall appoint in such manner as Congress may direct:

A number of electors of President and Vice President equal to the whole number of Senators and Representatives in Congress to which the District would be entitled if it were a State, but in no event more than the least populous State; they shall be in addition to those appointed by the States, but they shall be considered, for the purposes of the election of President and Vice President, to be electors appointed by a State; and they shall meet in the District and perform such duties as provided by the twelfth article of amendment.

Section 2.
The Congress shall have power to enforce this article by appropriate legislation.

AMENDMENT XXIV - Passed by Congress August 27, 1962. Ratified January 23, 1964.

Section 1.
The right of citizens of the United States to vote in any primary or other election for President or Vice President, for electors for President or Vice President, or for Senator or Representative in Congress, shall not be denied or abridged by the United States or any State by reason of failure to pay poll tax or other tax.

Section 2.
The Congress shall have power to enforce this article by appropriate legislation.

AMENDMENT XXV - Passed by Congress July 6, 1965. Ratified February 10, 1967.

Note: Article II, section 1, of the Constitution was affected by the 25th amendment.

Section 1.
In case of the removal of the President from office or of his death or resignation, the Vice President shall become President.

Section 2.
Whenever there is a vacancy in the office of the Vice President, the President shall nominate a Vice President who shall take office upon confirmation by a majority vote of both Houses of Congress.

Section 3.
Whenever the President transmits to the President pro tempore of the Senate and the Speaker of the House of Representatives his written declaration that he is unable to discharge the powers and duties of his office, and until he transmits to them a written declaration to the contrary, such powers and duties shall be discharged by the Vice President as Acting President.

Section 4.
Whenever the Vice President and a majority of either the principal officers of the executive departments or of such other body as Congress may by law provide, transmit to the President pro tempore of the Senate and the Speaker of the House of Representatives their written declaration that the President is unable to discharge the powers and duties of his office, the Vice President shall immediately assume the powers and duties of the office as Acting President.

Thereafter, when the President transmits to the President pro tempore of the Senate and the Speaker of the House of Representatives his written declaration that no inability exists, he shall resume the powers and duties of his office unless the Vice President and a majority of either the principal officers of the executive department or of such other body as Congress may by law provide, transmit within four days to the President pro tempore of the Senate and the Speaker of the House of Representatives their written declaration that the President is unable to discharge the powers and duties of his office. Thereupon Congress shall decide the issue, assembling within forty-eight hours for that purpose if not in session. If the Congress, within twenty-one days after receipt of the latter written declaration, or, if Congress is not in session, within twenty-one days after Congress is required to assemble, determines by two-thirds vote of both Houses that the President is unable to discharge the powers and duties of his office, the Vice President shall continue to discharge the same as Acting President; otherwise, the President shall resume the powers and duties of his office.

AMENDMENT XXVI - Passed by Congress March 23, 1971. Ratified July 1, 1971.

Note: Amendment 14, section 2, of the Constitution was modified by section 1 of the 26th amendment.

Section 1.
The right of citizens of the United States, who are eighteen years of age or older, to vote shall not **be denied or abridged by the United States or by any State on account of age.**

Section 2.
The Congress shall have power to enforce this article by appropriate legislation.

AMENDMENT XXVII - Originally proposed Sept. 25, 1789. Ratified May 7, 1992.

No law, varying the compensation for the services of the Senators and Representatives, shall take effect, until an election of representatives shall have intervened.

ARTICLES IN ADDITION TO, AND AMENDMENT OF, THE CONSTITUTION OF THE UNITED STATES OF AMERICA, PROPOSED BY CONGRESS, AND RATIFIED BY THE LEGISLATURES OF THE SEVERAL STATES, PURSUANT TO THE FIFTH ARTICLE OF THE ORIGINAL CONSTITUTION

ARTICLE [I.]

Congress shall make no law respecting an establishment of religion, or prohibiting the free exercise thereof; or abridging the freedom of speech, or of the press; of the right of the people peaceably to assemble, and to petition the Government for a redress of grievances.

ARTICLE [II.]

A well-regulated Militia, being necessary to the security of a Free State, the right of the people to keep and bear Arms, shall not be infringed.

ARTICLE [III.]

No Soldier shall, in time of peace be quartered in any house, without the consent of the Owner, nor in time of war, but in a manner to be prescribed by law.

ARTICLE [IV.]

The right of the people to be secure in their persons, houses, papers, and effects, against unreasonable searches and seizures, shall not be violated, and no Warrants shall issue, but upon probable cause, supported by Oath or affirmation, and particularly describing the place to be searched, and the persons or things to be seized.

ARTICLE [V.]

No person shall be held to answer for a capital, or otherwise infamous crime, unless on a presentment or indictment of a Grand Jury, except in cases arising in the land or naval forces, or in the Militia, when in actual service in time of War or public danger; nor shall any person be subject for the same offence to be twice put in jeopardy of life or limb; nor shall be compelled in any criminal case to be a witness against himself, nor be deprived of life, liberty, or property, without due process of law; nor shall private property be taken for public use, without just compensation.

ARTICLE [VI.]

In all criminal prosecutions, the accused shall enjoy the right to a speedy and public trial, by an impartial jury of the State and district wherein the crime shall have been committed, which district shall have been previously ascertained by law, and to be informed of the nature and cause of the accusation; to be confronted with the witnesses against him; to have compulsory process for obtaining witnesses in his favor, and to have the Assistance of Counsel for his defense.

ARTICLE [VII.]

In Suits at common law, where the value in controversy shall exceed twenty dollars, the right of trial by jury shall be preserved, and no fact tried by a jury, shall be otherwise re-examined in any Court of the United States, than according to the rules of the common law.

ARTICLE [VIII.]

Excessive bail shall not be required, nor excessive fines imposed, nor cruel and unusual punishments inflicted.

ARTICLE [IX.]

The enumeration in the Constitution, of certain rights, shall not be construed to deny or disparage others retained by the people.

ARTICLE [X.]

The powers not delegated to the United States by the Constitution, nor prohibited by it to the States, are reserved to the States respectively, or to the people.

ARTICLE [XI.]

The Judicial power of the United States shall not be construed to extend to any suit in law or equity, commenced or prosecuted against one of the United States by Citizens of another State, or by Citizens or Subjects of any Foreign State.

PROPOSAL AND RATIFICATION

The eleventh amendment to the Constitution of the United States was proposed to the legislatures of the several States by the Third Congress, on the 4th of March 1794; and was declared in a message from the President to Congress, dated the 8th of January, 1798, to have been ratified by the legislatures of three-fourths of the States. The dates of ratification were: New York, March 27, 1794; Rhode Island, March 31, 1794; Connecticut, May 8, 1794; New Hampshire, June 16, 1794; Massachusetts, June 26, 1794; Vermont, between October 9, 1794 and November 9, 1794; Virginia, November 18, 1794; Georgia, November 29, 1794; Kentucky, December 7,

VerDate Aug 31 2005 11:19 Dec 10, 2007 Jkt 036932 PO 00000 Frm 00020 Fmt 7601 Sfmt 7601 E:\HR\OC\932.CC 932 cprice-sewell on PROD1PC72 with HEARING This sentence has been superseded by section 3 of amendment XX.

1794; Maryland, December 26, 1794; Delaware, January 23, 1795; North Carolina, February 7, 1795. Ratification was completed on February 7, 1795. The amendment was subsequently ratified by South Carolina on December 4, 1797. New Jersey and Pennsylvania did not take action on the amendment.

ARTICLE [XII.]

The Electors shall meet in their respective states, and vote by ballot for President and Vice-President, one of whom, at least, shall not be an inhabitant of the same state with themselves; they shall name in their ballots the person voted for as President, and in distinct ballots the person voted for as Vice-President, and they shall make distinct lists of all persons voted for as President, and of all persons voted for as Vice-President, and of the number of votes for each, which lists they shall sign and certify, and transmit sealed to the seat of the government of the United States, directed to the President of the Senate;—The President of the Senate shall, in the presence of the Senate and House of Representatives, open all the certificates and the votes shall then be counted;—The person having the greatest number of votes for President, shall be the President, if such number be a majority of the whole number of Electors appointed; and if no person have such majority, then from the persons having the highest numbers not exceeding three on the list of those voted for as President, the House of Representatives shall choose immediately, by ballot, the President.

But in choosing the President, the votes shall be taken by states, the representation from each state having one vote; a quorum for this purpose shall consist of a member or members from two-thirds of the states, and a majority of all the states shall be necessary to a choice. And if the House of Representatives shall not choose a President whenever the right of choice shall devolve upon them, before the fourth day of March next following, then the Vice-President shall act as President, as in the case of the death or other constitutional disability of the President. The person having the greatest number of votes as Vice-President, shall be the Vice-President, if such number be a majority of the whole number of Electors appointed, and if no person have a majority, then from the two highest numbers on the list, the Senate shall choose the Vice-President; a quorum for the purpose shall consist of two-thirds of the whole number of Senators, and a majority of the whole number shall be necessary to a choice. But no person constitutionally ineligible to the office of President shall be eligible to that of Vice-President of the United States.

PROPOSAL AND RATIFICATION

The twelfth amendment to the Constitution of the United States was proposed to the legislatures of the several States by the Eighth Congress, on the 9th of December, 1803, in lieu of the original third paragraph of the first section of the second article; and was declared in a proclamation of the Secretary of State, dated the 25th of September, 1804, to have been ratified by the legislatures of 13 of the 17 States. The dates of ratification were: North Carolina, December 21, 1803; Maryland, December 24, 1803; Kentucky, December 27, 1803; Ohio, December 30, 1803; Pennsylvania, January 5, 1804; Vermont, January 30, 1804; Virginia, February 3, 1804; New York, February 10, 1804; New Jersey, February 22, 1804; Rhode Island, March 12, 1804; South Carolina, May 15, 1804; Georgia, May 19, 1804; New Hampshire, June 15, 1804. Ratification was completed on June 15, 1804. The amendment was subsequently ratified by Tennessee, July 27, 1804. The amendment was rejected by Delaware, January 18, 1804; Massachusetts, February 3, 1804; Connecticut, at its session begun May 10, 1804.
This sentence has been superseded by section 3 of amendment XX.

ARTICLE XIII.

SECTION 1. Neither slavery nor involuntary servitude, except as a punishment for crime whereof the party shall have been duly convicted, shall exist within the United States, or any place subject to their jurisdiction.

SECTION 2. Congress shall have power to enforce this article by appropriate legislation.

PROPOSAL AND RATIFICATION

The thirteenth amendment to the Constitution of the United States was proposed to the legislatures of the several States by the Thirty-eighth Congress, on the 31st day of January, 1865, and was declared, in a proclamation of the Secretary of State, dated the 18th of December, 1865, to have been ratified by the legislatures of twenty-seven of the thirty-six States. The dates of ratification were: Illinois, February 1, 1865; Rhode Island, February 2, 1865; Michigan, February 2, 1865; Maryland, February 3, 1865; New York, February 3, 1865; Pennsylvania, February 3, 1865; West Virginia, February 3, 1865; Missouri, February 6, 1865; Maine, February 7, 1865; Kansas, February 7, 1865; Massachusetts, February 7, 1865; Virginia, February 9, 1865; Ohio, February 10, 1865; Indiana, February 13, 1865; Nevada, February 16, 1865; Louisiana, February 17, 1865; Minnesota, February 23, 1865; Wisconsin, February 24, 1865; Vermont, March 9, 1865; Tennessee, April 7, 1865; Arkansas, April 14, 1865; Connecticut, May 4, 1865; New Hampshire, July 1, 1865; South Carolina, November 13, 1865; Alabama, December 2, 1865; North Carolina, December 4, 1865; Georgia, December 6, 1865. Ratification was completed on December 6, 1865. The amendment was subsequently ratified by Oregon, December 8, 1865; California, December 19, 1865; Florida, December 28, 1865 (Florida again ratified on June 9, 1868, upon its adoption of a new constitution); Iowa, January 15, 1866; New Jersey, January 23, 1866 (after having rejected the amendment on March 16, 1865); Texas, February 18, 1870; Delaware, February 12, 1901 (after having rejected the amendment on February 8, 1865); Kentucky, March 18, 1976 (after having rejected it on February 24, 1865). The amendment was rejected (and not subsequently ratified) by Mississippi, December 4, 1865.

ARTICLE XIV.

SECTION 1. All persons born or naturalized in the United States, and subject to the jurisdiction thereof, are citizens of the United States and of the State wherein they reside. No State shall make or enforce any law which shall abridge the privileges or immunities of citizens of the United States; nor shall any State deprive any person of life, liberty, or property, without due process of law; nor deny to any person within its jurisdiction the equal protection of the laws.

SECTION 2. Representatives shall be apportioned among the several States according to their respective numbers, counting the whole number of persons in each State, excluding Indians not taxed. But when the right to vote at any election for the choice of electors for President and Vice President of the United States, Representatives in Congress, the Executive and Judicial officers of a State, or the members of the

Legislature thereof, is denied to any of the male inhabitants of such State, being twenty-one years of age,15 and citizens of the United States, or in any way abridged, except for participation in rebellion, or other crime, the basis of representation therein shall be reduced in the proportion which the number of such male citizens shall bear to the whole number of male citizens twenty-one years of age in such State.

SECTION 3. No person shall be a Senator or Representative in Congress, or elector of President and Vice President, or hold any office, civil or military, under the United States, or under any State, who, having previously taken an oath, as a member of Congress, or as an officer of the United States, or as a member of any State legislature, or as an executive or judicial officer of any State, to support the Constitution of the United States, shall have engaged in insurrection or rebellion against the same, or given aid or comfort to the enemies thereof. But Congress may by a vote of two- thirds of each House, remove such disability.

SECTION 4. The validity of the public debt of the United States, authorized by law, including debts incurred for payment of pensions and bounties for services in suppressing insurrection or rebellion, shall not be questioned. But neither the United States nor any State shall assume or pay any debt or obligation incurred in aid of insurrection or rebellion against the United States, or any claim for the loss or emancipation of any slave; but all such debts, obligations and claims shall be held illegal and void.

SECTION 5. The Congress shall have power to enforce, by appropriate legislation, the provisions of this article.

PROPOSAL AND RATIFICATION

The fourteenth amendment to the Constitution of the United States was proposed to the legislatures of the several States by the Thirty-ninth Congress, on the 13th of June, 1866. It was declared, in a certificate of the Secretary of State dated July 28, 1868 to have been ratified by the legislatures of 28 of the 37 States. The dates of ratification were: Connecticut, June 25, 1866; New Hampshire, July 6, 1866; Tennessee, July 19, 1866; New Jersey, September 11, 1866 (subsequently the legislature rescinded its ratification, and on March 24, 1868, readopted its resolution of rescission over the Governor's veto, and on November 12, 1980, expressed support for the amendment); Oregon, September 19, 1866 (and rescinded its ratification on October 15, 1868); Vermont, October 30, 1866; Ohio, January 4, 1867 (and rescinded its ratification on January 15, 1868); New York, January 10, 1867; Kansas, January 11, 1867; Illinois, January 15, 1867; West Virginia, January 16, 1867; Michigan, January 16, 1867; Minnesota, January 16, 1867; Maine, January 19, 1867; Nevada, January 22, 1867; Indiana, January 23, 1867; Missouri, January 25, 1867; Rhode Island, February 7, 1867; Wisconsin, February 7, 1867; Pennsylvania, February 12, 1867; Massachusetts, March 20, 1867; Nebraska, June 15, 1867; Iowa, March 16, 1868; Arkansas, April 6, 1868; Florida, June 9, 1868; North Carolina, July 4, 1868 (after having rejected it on December 14, 1866); Louisiana, July 9, 1868 (after having rejected it on February 6, 1867); South Carolina, July 9, 1868 (after having rejected it on December 20, 1866). Ratification was completed on July 9, 1868. The amendment was subsequently ratified by Alabama, July 13, 1868; Georgia, July 21, 1868 (after having rejected it on November 9, 1866); Virginia, October 8, 1869 (after having rejected it on January 9, 1867); Mississippi, January 17, 1870; Texas, February 18, 1870 (after having rejected it on October 27, 1866); Delaware, February 12, 1901 (after having rejected it on February 8, 1867); Maryland, April 4, 1959 (after having rejected it on March 23, 1867); California, May 6, 1959; Kentucky, March 18, 1976 (after having rejected it on January 8, 1867).

See amendment XIX and section 1 of amendment XXVI.

ARTICLE XV.

SECTION 1. The right of citizens of the United States to vote shall not be denied or abridged by the United States or by any State on account of race, color, or previous condition of servitude.

SECTION 2. The Congress shall have power to enforce this article by appropriate legislation.

PROPOSAL AND RATIFICATION

The fifteenth amendment to the Constitution of the United States was proposed to the legislatures of the several States by the Fortieth Congress, on the 26th of February, 1869, and was declared, in a proclamation of the Secretary of State, dated March 30, 1870, to have been ratified by the legislatures of twenty-nine of the thirty-seven States. The dates of ratification were: Nevada, March 1, 1869; West Virginia, March 3, 1869; Illinois, March 5, 1869; Louisiana, March 5, 1869; North Carolina, March 5, 1869; Michigan, March 8, 1869; Wisconsin, March 9, 1869; Maine, March 11, 1869; Massachusetts, March 12, 1869; Arkansas, March 15, 1869; South Carolina, March 15, 1869; Pennsylvania, March 25, 1869; New York, April 14, 1869 (and the legislature of the same State passed a resolution January 5, 1870, to withdraw its consent to it, which action it rescinded on March 30, 1970); Indiana, May 14, 1869; Connecticut, May 19, 1869; Florida, June 14, 1869; New Hampshire, July 1, 1869; Virginia, October 8, 1869; Vermont, October 20, 1869; Missouri, January 7, 1870; Minnesota, January 13, 1870; Mississippi, January 17, 1870; Rhode Island, January 18, 1870; Kansas, January 19, 1870; Ohio, January 27, 1870 (after having rejected it on April 30, 1869); Georgia, February 2, 1870; Iowa, February 3, 1870. Ratification was completed on February 3, 1870, unless the withdrawal of ratification by New York was effective; in which event ratification was completed on February 17, 1870, when Nebraska ratified. The amendment was subsequently ratified by Texas, February 18, 1870; New Jersey, February 15, 1871 (after having rejected it on February 7, 1870); Delaware, February 12, 1901 (after having rejected it on March 18, 1869); Oregon, February 24, 1959; California, April 3, 1962 (after having rejected it on January 28, 1870); Kentucky, March 18, 1976 (after having rejected it on March 12, 1869); Tennessee, April 8, 1997 (after having rejected it on November 16, 1869). The amendment was approved by the Governor of Maryland, May 7, 1973; Maryland having previously rejected it on February 26, 1870.

ARTICLE XVI.

The Congress shall have power to lay and collect taxes on incomes, from whatever source derived, without apportionment among the several States, and without regard to any census or enumeration.

PROPOSAL AND RATIFICATION

The sixteenth amendment to the Constitution of the United States was proposed to the legislatures of the several States by the Sixty-first Congress on the 12th of July, 1909, and was declared, in a proclamation of the Secretary of State, dated the 25th of February, 1913, to have been ratified by 36 of the 48 States. The dates of ratification were: Alabama, August 10, 1909; Kentucky, February 8, 1910; South Carolina, February 19, 1910; Illinois, March 1, 1910; Mississippi, March 7, 1910; Oklahoma, March 10, 1910; Maryland, April 8, 1910; Georgia, August 3, 1910; Texas, August 16, 1910; Ohio, January 19, 1911; Idaho, January 20, 1911; Oregon, January 23, 1911; Washington, January 26, 1911; Montana, January 30, 1911; Indiana, January 30, 1911; California, January 31, 1911; Nevada, January 31, 1911; South Dakota, February 3, 1911; Nebraska, February 9, 1911; North Carolina, February 11, 1911; Colorado, February 15, 1911; North Dakota, February 17, 1911; Kansas, February 18, 1911; Michigan, February 23, 1911; Iowa, February 24, 1911; Missouri, March 16, 1911; Maine, March 31, 1911; Tennessee, April 7, 1911; Arkansas, April 22, 1911 (after having rejected it earlier); Wisconsin, May 26, 1911; New York, July 12, 1911; Arizona, April 6, 1912; Minnesota, June 11, 1912; Louisiana, June 28, 1912; West Virginia, January 31, 1913; New Mexico, February 3, 1913. Ratification was completed on February 3, 1913.

VerDate Aug 31 2005 11:19 Dec 10, 2007 Jkt 036932 PO 00000 Frm 00024 Fmt 7601 Sfmt 7601 E:\

The amendment was subsequently ratified by Massachusetts, March 4, 1913; New Hampshire, March 7, 1913 (after having rejected it on March 2, 1911). The amendment was rejected (and not subsequently ratified) by Connecticut, Rhode Island, and Utah.

ARTICLE [XVII.]

The Senate of the United States shall be composed of two Senators from each State, elected by the people thereof, for six years; and each Senator shall have one vote. The electors in each State shall have the qualifications requisite for electors of the most numerous branch of the State legislatures. When vacancies happen in the representation of any State in the Senate, the executive authority of such State shall issue writs of election to fill such vacancies: Provided, that the legislature of any State may empower the executive thereof to make temporary appointments until the people fill the vacancies by election as the legislature may direct. This amendment shall not be so construed as to affect the election or term of any Senator chosen before it becomes valid as part of the Constitution.

PROPOSAL AND RATIFICATION

The seventeenth amendment to the Constitution of the United States was proposed to the legislatures of the several States by the Sixty-second Congress on the 13th of May, 1912, and was declared, in a proclamation of the Secretary of State, dated the 31st of May, 1913, to have been ratified by the legislatures of 36 of the 48 States. The dates of ratification were:

Massachusetts, May 22, 1912; Arizona, June 3, 1912; Minnesota, June 10, 1912; New York, January 15, 1913; Kansas, January 17, 1913; Oregon, January 23, 1913; North Carolina, January 25, 1913; California, January 28, 1913; Michigan, January 28, 1913; Iowa, January 30, 1913; Montana, January 30, 1913; Idaho, January 31, 1913; West Virginia, February 4, 1913; Colorado, February 5, 1913; Nevada, February 6, 1913; Texas, February 7, 1913; Washington, February 7, 1913; Wyoming, February 8, 1913; Arkansas, February 11, 1913; Maine, February 11, 1913; Illinois, February 13, 1913; North Dakota, February 14, 1913; Wisconsin, February 18, 1913; Indiana, February 19, 1913; New Hampshire, February 19, 1913; Vermont, February 19, 1913; South Dakota, February 19, 1913; Oklahoma, February 24, 1913; Ohio, February 25, 1913; Missouri, March 7, 1913; New Mexico, March 13, 1913; Nebraska, March 14, 1913; New Jersey, March 17, 1913; Tennessee, April 1, 1913; Pennsylvania, April 2, 1913; Connecticut, April 8, 1913. Ratification was completed on April 8, 1913. The amendment was subsequently ratified by Louisiana, June 11, 1914. The amendment was rejected by Utah (and not subsequently ratified) on February 26, 1913.

ARTICLE [XVIII.]

SECTION 1. After one year from the ratification of this article the manufacture, sale, or transportation of intoxicating liquors within, the importation thereof into, or the exportation thereof from the United States and all territory subject to the jurisdiction thereof for beverage purposes is hereby prohibited.

SECTION 2. The Congress and the several States shall have concurrent power to enforce this article by appropriate legislation.

SECTION 3. This article shall be inoperative unless it shall have been ratified as an amendment to the Constitution by the legislatures of the several States, as provided in the Constitution, within seven years from the date of the submission hereof to the States by the Congress.

PROPOSAL AND RATIFICATION

The eighteenth amendment to the Constitution of the United States was proposed to the legislatures of the several States by the Sixty-fifth Congress, on the 18th of December, 1917, and was declared, in a proclamation of the Secretary of State, dated the 29th of January, 1919, to have been ratified by the legislatures of 36 of the 48 States. The dates of ratification were: Mississippi, January 8, 1918; Virginia, January 11, 1918; Kentucky, January 14, 1918; North Dakota, January 25, 1918; South Carolina, January 29, 1918; Maryland, February 13, 1918; Montana, February 19, 1918; Texas, March 4, 1918; Delaware, March 18, 1918; South Dakota, March 20, 1918; Massachusetts, April 2, 1918; Arizona, May 24, 1918; Georgia, June 26, 1918; Louisiana, August 3, 1918; Florida, December 3, 1918; Michigan, January 2, 1919; Ohio, January 7, 1919; Oklahoma, January 7, 1919;

Idaho, January 8, 1919; Maine, January 8, 1919; West Virginia, January 9, 1919; California, January 13, 1919; Tennessee, January 13, 1919; Washington, January 13, 1919; Arkansas, January 14, 1919; Kansas, January 14, 1919; Alabama, January 15, 1919; Colorado, January 15, 1919; Iowa, January 15, 1919; New Hampshire, January 15, 1919; Oregon, January 15, 1919; Nebraska, January 16, 1919; North Carolina, January 16, 1919; Utah, January 16, 1919; Missouri, January 16, 1919; Wyoming, January 16, 1919. Ratification was completed on January 16, 1919. See Dillon v. Gloss, 256 U.S. 368, 376 (1921). The amendment was subsequently ratified by Minnesota on January 17, 1919; Wisconsin, January 17, 1919; New Mexico, January 20, 1919; Nevada, January 21, 1919; New York, January 29, 1919; Vermont, January 29, 1919; Pennsylvania, February 25, 1919; Connecticut, May 6, 1919; and New Jersey, March 9, 1922. The amendment was rejected (and not subsequently ratified) by Rhode Island.

ARTICLE [XIX.]

The right of citizens of the United States to vote shall not be denied or abridged by the United States or by any State on account of sex. Congress shall have power to enforce this article by appropriate legislation.

PROPOSAL AND RATIFICATION

The nineteenth amendment to the Constitution of the United States was proposed to the legislatures of the several States by the Sixty-sixth Congress, on the 4th of June, 1919, and was declared, in a proclamation of the Secretary of State, dated the 26th of August, 1920, to have been ratified by the legislatures of 36 of the 48 States. The dates of ratification were: Illinois, June 10, 1919 (and that State readopted its resolution of ratification June 17, 1919); Michigan, June 10, 1919; Wisconsin, June 10, 1919; Kansas, June 16, 1919; New York, June 16, 1919; Ohio, June 16, 1919; Pennsylvania, June 24, 1919; Massachusetts, June 25, 1919; Texas, June 28, 1919; Iowa, July 2, 1919; Missouri, July 3, 1919; Arkansas, July 28, 1919; Montana, August 2, 1919; Nebraska, August 2, 1919; Minnesota, September 8, 1919; New Hampshire, September 10, 1919; Utah, October 2, 1919; California, November 1, 1919; Maine, November 5, 1919; North Dakota, December 1, 1919; South Dakota, December 4, 1919; Colorado, December 15, 1919; Kentucky, January 6, 1920; Rhode Island, January 6, 1920; Oregon, January 13, 1920; Indiana, January 16, 1920; Wyoming, January 27, 1920; Nevada, February 7, 1920; New Jersey, February 9, 1920; Idaho, February 11, 1920; Arizona, February 12, 1920; New Mexico, February 21, 1920; Oklahoma, February 28, 1920; West Virginia, March 10, 1920; Washington, March 22, 1920; Tennessee, August 18, 1920. Ratification was completed on August 18, 1920. The amendment was subsequently ratified by Connecticut on September 14, 1920 (and that State reaffirmed it on September 21, 1920); Vermont, February 8, 1921; Delaware, March 6, 1923 (after having rejected it on June 2, 1920); Maryland, March 29, 1941 (after having rejected it on February 24, 1920, ratification certified on February 25, 1958); Virginia, February 21, 1952 (after having rejected it on February 12, 1920); Alabama, September 8, 1953 (after having rejected it on September 22, 1919); Florida, May 13, 1969; South Carolina, July 1, 1969 (after having rejected it on January 28, 1920, ratification certified on August 22, 1973); Georgia, February 20, 1970 (after having rejected it on July 24, 1919); Louisiana, June 11, 1970 (after having rejected it on July 1, 1920); North Carolina, May 6, 1971; Mississippi, March 22, 1984 (after having rejected it on March 29, 1920).

ARTICLE [XX.]

SECTION 1. The terms of the President and Vice President shall end at noon on the 20th day of January, and the terms of Senators and Representatives at noon on the 3d day of January, of the years in which such terms would have ended if this article had not been ratified; and the terms of their successors shall then begin.

SECTION 2. The Congress shall assemble at least once in every year, and such meeting shall begin at noon on the 3d day of January, unless they shall by law appoint a different day.

SECTION 3. If, at the time fixed for the beginning of the term of the President, the President elect shall have died, the Vice President elect shall become President. If a President shall not have been chosen before the time fixed for the beginning of his term, or if the President elect shall have failed to qualify, then the Vice President elect shall act as President until a President shall have qualified; and the Congress may by law provide for the case wherein neither a President elect nor a Vice President elect shall have qualified, declaring who shall then act as President, or the manner in which one who is to act shall be selected, and such person shall act accordingly until a President or Vice President shall have qualified.

SECTION 4. The Congress may by law provide for the case of the death of any of the persons from whom the House of Representatives may choose a President whenever the right of choice shall have devolved upon them, and for the case of the death of any of the persons from whom the Senate may choose a Vice President whenever the right of choice shall have devolved upon them.

SECTION 5. Sections 1 and 2 shall take effect on the 15th day of October following the ratification of this article.

SECTION 6. This article shall be inoperative unless it shall have been ratified as an amendment to the Constitution by the legislatures of three-fourths of the several States within seven years from the date of its submission.

PROPOSAL AND RATIFICATION

The twentieth amendment to the Constitution was proposed to the legislatures of the several states by the Seventy-Second Congress, on the 2d day of March, 1932, and was declared, in a proclamation by the Secretary of State, dated on the 6th day of February, 1933, to have been ratified by the legislatures of 36 of the 48 States. The dates of ratification were: Virginia, March 4, 1932; New York, March 11, 1932; Mississippi, March 16, 1932; Arkansas, March 17, 1932; Kentucky, March 17, 1932; New Jersey, March 21, 1932; South Carolina, March 25, 1932; Michigan, March 31, 1932; Maine, April 1, 1932; Rhode Island, April 14, 1932; Illinois, April 21, 1932; Louisiana, June 22, 1932; West Virginia, July 30, 1932; Pennsylvania, August 11, 1932; Indiana, August 15, 1932; Texas, September 7, 1932;

Alabama, September 13, 1932; California, January 4, 1933; North Carolina, January 5, 1933; North Dakota, January 9,1933; Minnesota, January 12, 1933; Arizona, January 13, 1933; Montana, January 13,1933; Nebraska, January 13, 1933; Oklahoma, January 13, 1933; Kansas, January 16, 1933; Oregon, January 16, 1933; Delaware, January 19, 1933; Washington, January 19, 1933; Wyoming, January 19, 1933; Iowa, January 20, 1933; South Dakota, January 20, 1933; Tennessee, January 20, 1933; Idaho, January 21, 1933; New Mexico, January 21, 1933; Georgia, January 23, 1933; Missouri, January 23, 1933; Ohio, January 23, 1933; Utah, January 23, 1933. Ratification was completed on January 23, 1933. Vermont, February 2, 1933; Maryland, March 24, 1933; Florida, April 26, 1933.

ARTICLE [XXI.]

SECTION 1. The eighteenth article of amendment to the Constitution of the United States is hereby repealed.

SECTION 2. The transportation or importation into any State, Territory, or possession of the United States for delivery or use therein of intoxicating liquors, in violation of the laws thereof, is hereby prohibited.

SECTION 3. This article shall be inoperative unless it shall have been ratified as an amendment to the Constitution by conventions in the several States, as provided in the Constitution, within seven years from the date of the submission hereof to the States by the Congress.

PROPOSAL AND RATIFICATION

The twenty-first amendment to the Constitution was proposed to the several states by the Seventy-Second Congress, on the 20th day of February, 1933, and was declared, in a proclamation by the Secretary of State, dated on the 5th day of December, 1933, to have been ratified by 36 of the 48 States. The dates of ratification were: Michigan, April 10, 1933; Wisconsin, April 25, 1933; Rhode Island, May 8, 1933; Wyoming, May 25, 1933; New Jersey, June 1, 1933; Delaware, June 24, 1933; Indiana, June 26, 1933; Massachusetts, June 26, 1933; New York, June 27, 1933; Illinois, July 10, 1933; Iowa, July 10, 1933; Connecticut, July 11, 1933; New Hampshire, July 11, 1933; California, July 24, 1933; West Virginia, July 25, 1933; Arkansas, August 1, 1933; Oregon, August 7, 1933; Alabama, August 8, 1933; Tennessee, August 11, 1933; Missouri, August 29, 1933; Arizona, September 5, 1933; Nevada, September 5, 1933; Vermont, September 23, 1933; Colorado, September 26, 1933; Washington, October 3, 1933; Minnesota, October 10, 1933; Idaho, October 17, 1933; Maryland, October 18, 1933; Virginia, October 25, 1933; New Mexico, November 2, 1933; Florida, November 14, 1933; Texas, November 24, 1933; Kentucky, November 27, 1933; Ohio, December 5, 1933; Pennsylvania, December 5, 1933; Utah, December 5, 1933. Ratification was completed on December 5, 1933. The amendment was subsequently ratified by Maine, on December 6, 1933, and by Montana, on August 6, 1934. The amendment was rejected (and not subsequently ratified) by South Carolina, on December 4, 1933.

ARTICLE [XXII.]

SECTION 1. No person shall be elected to the office of the President more than twice, and no person who has held the office of President, or acted as President, for more than two years of a term of which some other person was elected President shall be elected to the office of the President more than once. But this Article shall not apply to any person holding the office of President when this Article was proposed by the Congress, and shall not prevent any person who may be holding the office of President, or acting as President, during the term within which this Article becomes operative from holding the office of President or acting as President during the remainder of such term.

SECTION 2. This article shall be inoperative unless it shall have been ratified as an amendment to the Constitution by the legislatures of three-fourths of the several States within seven years from the date of its submission to the States by the Congress. **PROPOSAL AND RATIFICATION**

This amendment was proposed to the legislatures of the several States by the Eightieth Congress on March 21, 1947 by House Joint Res. No. 27, and was declared by the Administrator of General Services, on March 1, 1951, to have been ratified by the legislatures of 36 of the 48 States. The dates of ratification were: Maine, March 31, 1947; Michigan, March 31, 1947; Iowa, April 1, 1947; Kansas, April 1, 1947; New Hampshire, April 1, 1947; Delaware, April 2, 1947; Illinois, April 3, 1947; Oregon, April 3, 1947; Colorado, April 12, 1947; California, April 15, 1947; New Jersey, April 15, 1947; Vermont, April 15, 1947; Ohio, April 16, 1947; Wisconsin, April 16, 1947; Pennsylvania, April 29, 1947; Connecticut, May 21, 1947; Missouri, May 22, 1947; Nebraska, May 23, 1947; Virginia, January 28, 1948; Mississippi, February 12, 1948; New York, March 9, 1948; South Dakota, January 21, 1949; North Dakota, February 25, 1949; Louisiana, May 17, 1950; Montana, January 25, 1951; Indiana, January 29, 1951; Idaho, January 30, 1951; New Mexico, February 12, 1951; Wyoming, February 12, 1951; Arkansas, February 15, 1951; Georgia, February 17, 1951; Tennessee, February 20, 1951; Texas, February 22, 1951; Nevada, February 26, 1951; Utah, February 26, 1951; Minnesota, February 27, 1951. Ratification was completed on February 27, 1951. The amendment was subsequently ratified by North Carolina on February 28, 1951; South Carolina, March 13, 1951; Maryland, March 14, 1951; Florida, April 16, 1951; Alabama, May 4, 1951. The amendment was rejected (and not subsequently ratified) by Oklahoma in June 1947, and Massachusetts on June 9, 1949. CERTIFICATION OF VALIDITY Publication of the certifying statement of the Administrator of General Services that the amendment had become valid was made on March 1, 1951, F.R. Doc. 51– 2940, 16 F.R. 2019.

ARTICLE [XXIII.]

SECTION 1. The District constituting the seat of Government of the United States shall appoint in such manner as the Congress may direct: A number of electors of

President and Vice President equal to the whole number of Senators and Representatives in Congress to which the District would be entitled if it were a State, but in no event more than the least populous State; they shall be in addition to those appointed by the States, but they shall be considered, for the purposes of the election of President and Vice President, to be electors appointed by a State; and they shall meet in the District and perform such duties as provided by the twelfth article of amendment.

SECTION 2. The Congress shall have power to enforce this article by appropriate legislation.

PROPOSAL AND RATIFICATION

This amendment was proposed by the Eighty-sixth Congress on June 17, 1960 and was declared by the Administrator of General Services on April 3, 1961, to have been ratified by 38 of the 50 States. The dates of ratification were: Hawaii, June 23, 1960 (and that State made a technical correction to its resolution on June 30, 1960); Massachusetts, August 22, 1960; New Jersey, December 19, 1960; New York, January 17, 1961; California, January 19, 1961; Oregon, January 27, 1961; Maryland, January 30, 1961; Idaho, January 31, 1961; Maine, January 31, 1961; Minnesota, January 31, 1961; New Mexico, February 1, 1961; Nevada, February 2, 1961; Montana, February 6, 1961; South Dakota, February 6, 1961; Colorado, February 8, 1961; Washington, February 9, 1961; West Virginia, February 9, 1961; Alaska, February 10, 1961; Wyoming, February 13, 1961; Delaware, February 20, 1961; Utah, February 21, 1961; Wisconsin, February 21, 1961; Pennsylvania, February 28, 1961; Indiana, March 3, 1961; North Dakota, March 3, 1961; Tennessee, March 6, 1961; Michigan, March 8, 1961; Connecticut, March 9, 1961; Arizona, March 10, 1961; Illinois, March 14, 1961; Nebraska, March 15, 1961; Vermont, March 15, 1961;

VerDate Aug 31 2005 11:19 Dec 10, 2007 Jkt 036932 PO 00000 Frm 00029 Fmt 7601 Sfmt 7601 E:\HR\OC\932.CC 932 cprice-sewell on PROD1PC72 with HEARING

Iowa, March 16, 1961; Missouri, March 20, 1961; Oklahoma, March 21, 1961; Rhode Island, March 22, 1961; Kansas, March 29, 1961; Ohio, March 29, 1961. Ratification was completed on March 29, 1961. The amendment was subsequently ratified by New Hampshire on March 30, 1961 (when that State annulled and then repeated its ratification of March 29, 1961). The amendment was rejected (and not subsequently ratified) by Arkansas on January 24, 1961. CERTIFICATION OF VALIDITY Publication of the certifying statement of the Administrator of General Services that the amendment had become valid was made on April 3, 1961, F.R. Doc. 61– 3017, 26 F.R. 2808.

ARTICLE [XXIV.]

SECTION 1. The right of citizens of the United States to vote in any primary or other election for President or Vice President, for electors for President or Vice President, or for Senator or Representative in Congress, shall not be denied or abridged by the United States or any State by reason of failure to pay any poll tax or other tax.

SECTION 2. The Congress shall have power to enforce this article by appropriate legislation.

PROPOSAL AND RATIFICATION

This amendment was proposed by the Eighty-seventh Congress by Senate Joint Resolution No. 29, which was approved by the Senate on March 27, 1962, and by the House of Representatives on August 27, 1962. It was declared by the Administrator of General Services on February 4, 1964, to have been ratified by the legislatures of 38 of the 50 States. This amendment was ratified by the following States: Illinois, November 14, 1962; New Jersey, December 3, 1962; Oregon, January 25, 1963; Montana, January 28, 1963; West Virginia, February 1, 1963; New York, February 4, 1963; Maryland, February 6, 1963; California, February 7, 1963; Alaska, February 11, 1963; Rhode Island, February 14, 1963; Indiana, February 19, 1963; Utah, February 20, 1963; Michigan, February 20, 1963; Colorado, February 21, 1963; Ohio, February 27, 1963; Minnesota, February 27, 1963; New Mexico, March 5, 1963; Hawaii, March 6, 1963; North Dakota, March 7, 1963; Idaho, March 8, 1963; Washington, March 14, 1963; Vermont, March 15, 1963; Nevada, March 19, 1963; Connecticut, March 20, 1963; Tennessee, March 21, 1963; Pennsylvania, March 25, 1963; Wisconsin, March 26, 1963; Kansas, March 28, 1963; Massachusetts, March 28, 1963; Nebraska, April 4, 1963; Florida, April 18, 1963; Iowa, April 24, 1963; Delaware, May 1, 1963; Missouri, May 13, 1963; New Hampshire, June 12, 1963; Kentucky, June 27, 1963; Maine, January 16, 1964; South Dakota, January 23, 1964; Virginia, February 25, 1977. Ratification was completed on January 23, 1964. The amendment was subsequently ratified by North Carolina on May 3, 1989. The amendment was rejected by Mississippi (and not subsequently ratified) on December 20, 1962.

CERTIFICATION OF VALIDITY

Publication of the certifying statement of the Administrator of General Services that the amendment had become valid was made on February 5, 1964, F.R. Doc. 64–1229, 29 F.R. 1715.

ARTICLE [XXV.]

SECTION 1. In case of the removal of the President from office or of his death or resignation, the Vice President shall become President.

SECTION 2. Whenever there is a vacancy in the office of the Vice President, the President shall nominate a Vice President who shall

VerDate Aug 31 2005 11:19 Dec 10, 2007 Jkt 036932 PO 00000 Frm 00030 Fmt 7601 Sfmt 7601
E:\HR\OC\932.CC 932 cprice-sewell on PROD1PC72 with HEARING

So in original. Probably should be "departments".

take office upon confirmation by a majority vote of both Houses of Congress.

SECTION 3. Whenever the President transmits to the President pro tempore of the Senate and the Speaker of the House of Representatives his written declaration that he is unable to discharge the powers and duties of his office, and until he transmits to them a written declaration to the contrary, such powers and duties shall be discharged by the Vice President as Acting President.

SECTION 4. Whenever the Vice President and a majority of either the principal officers of the executive departments or of such other body as Congress may by law provide, transmit to the President pro tempore of the Senate and the Speaker of the House of Representatives their written declaration that the President is unable to discharge the powers and duties of his office, the Vice President shall immediately assume the powers and duties of the office as Acting President. Thereafter, when the President transmits to the President pro tempore of the Senate and the Speaker of the House of Representatives his written declaration that no inability exists, he shall resume the powers and duties of his office unless the Vice President and a majority of either the principal officers of the executive department17 or of such other body as Congress may by law provide, transmit within four days to the President pro tempore of the Senate and the Speaker of the House of Representatives their written declaration that the President is unable to discharge the powers and duties of his office. Thereupon Congress shall decide the issue, assembling within forty-eight hours for that purpose if not in session. If the Congress, within twenty-one days after receipt of the latter written declaration, or, if Congress is not in session, within twenty-one days after Congress is required to assemble, determines by two-thirds vote of both Houses that the President is unable to discharge the powers and duties of his office, the Vice President shall continue to discharge the same as Acting President; otherwise, the President shall resume the powers and duties of his office.

PROPOSAL AND RATIFICATION

This amendment was proposed by the Eighty-ninth Congress by Senate Joint Resolution No. 1, which was approved by the Senate on February 19, 1965, and by the House of Representatives, in amended form, on April 13, 1965. The House of Representatives agreed to a Conference Report on June 30, 1965, and the Senate agreed to the Conference Report on July 6, 1965. It was declared by the Administrator of General Services, on February 23, 1967, to have been ratified by the legislatures of 39 of the 50 States. This amendment was ratified by the following States: Nebraska, July 12, 1965; Wisconsin, July 13, 1965; Oklahoma, July 15, 1965; Massachusetts, August 9, 1965; Pennsylvania, August 18, 1965; Kentucky, September 15, 1965; Arizona, September 22, 1965; Michigan, October 5, 1965; Indiana, October 20, 1965; California, October 21, 1965; Arkansas, November 4, 1965; New Jersey, November 29, 1965; Delaware, December 7, 1965; Utah, January 17, 1966; West Virginia, January 20, 1966; Maine, January 24, 1966; Rhode Island, January 28, 1966; Colorado, February 3, 1966; New Mexico, February 3, 1966; Kansas, February 8, 1966; Vermont, February 10, 1966; Alaska, February 18, 1966; Idaho, March 2, 1966; Hawaii, March 3, 1966; Virginia, March 8, 1966; Mississippi, March 10, 1966; New York, March 14, 1966; Maryland, March 23, 1966; Missouri, March 30, 1966; New

Hampshire, June 13, 1966; Louisiana, July 5, 1966; Tennessee, January 12, 1967; Wyoming, January 25, 1967; Washington, January 26, 1967; Iowa, January 26, 1967; Oregon, February 2, 1967; Minnesota, February 10, 1967; Nevada, February 10, 1967. Ratification was completed on February 10, 1967. The amendment was subsequently ratified by Connecticut, February 14, 1967; Montana, February 15, 1967; South Dakota, March 6, 1967; Ohio, March 7, 1967; Alabama, March 14, 1967; North Carolina, March 22, 1967; Illinois, March 22, 1967; Texas, April 25, 1967; Florida, May 25, 1967.

CERTIFICATION OF VALIDITY

Publication of the certifying statement of the Administrator of General Services that the amendment had become valid was made on February 25, 1967, F.R. Doc. 67–2208, 32 F.R. 3287.

ARTICLE [XXVI.]

SECTION 1. The right of citizens of the United States, who are eighteen years of age or older, to vote shall not be denied or abridged by the United States or by any State on account of age.

SECTION 2. The Congress shall have power to enforce this article by appropriate legislation.

PROPOSAL AND RATIFICATION

This amendment was proposed by the Ninety-second Congress by Senate Joint Resolution No. 7, which was approved by the Senate on March 10, 1971, and by the House of Representatives on March 23, 1971. It was declared by the Administrator of General Services on July 5, 1971, to have been ratified by the legislature of 39 of the 50 States. This amendment was ratified by the following States: Connecticut, March 23, 1971; Delaware, March 23, 1971; Minnesota, March 23, 1971; Tennessee, March 23, 1971; Washington, March 23, 1971; Hawaii, March 24, 1971; Massachusetts, March 24, 1971; Montana, March 29, 1971; Arkansas, March 30, 1971; Idaho, March 30, 1971; Iowa, March 30, 1971; Nebraska, April 2, 1971; New Jersey, April 3, 1971; Kansas, April 7, 1971; Michigan, April 7, 1971; Alaska, April 8, 1971; Maryland, April 8, 1971; Indiana, April 8, 1971; Maine, April 9, 1971; Vermont, April 16, 1971; Louisiana, April 17, 1971; California, April 19, 1971; Colorado, April 27, 1971; Pennsylvania, April 27, 1971; Texas, April 27, 1971; South Carolina, April 28, 1971; West Virginia, April 28, 1971; New Hampshire, May 13, 1971; Arizona, May 14, 1971; Rhode Island, May 27, 1971; New York, June 2, 1971; Oregon, June 4, 1971; Missouri, June 14, 1971; Wisconsin, June 22, 1971; Illinois, June 29, 1971; Alabama, June 30, 1971; Ohio, June 30, 1971; North Carolina, July 1, 1971; Oklahoma, July 1, 1971. Ratification was completed on July 1, 1971. The amendment was subsequently ratified by Virginia, July 8, 1971; Wyoming, July 8, 1971; Georgia, October 4, 1971.

CERTIFICATION OF VALIDITY

Publication of the certifying statement of the Administrator of General Services that the amendment had become valid was made on July 7, 1971, F.R. Doc. 71– 9691, 36 F.R. 12725.

ARTICLE [XXVII.]

No law, varying the compensation for the services of the Senators and Representatives, shall take effect, until an election of Representatives shall have intervened.

PROPOSAL AND RATIFICATION

This amendment, being the second of twelve articles proposed by the First Congress on Sept. 25, 1789, was declared by the Archivist of the United States on May 18, 1992, to have been ratified by the legislatures of 40 of the 50 States. This amendment was ratified by the following States: Maryland, December 19, 1789; North Carolina, December 22, 1789; South Carolina, January 19, 1790; Delaware, January 28, 1790; Vermont, November 3, 1791; Virginia, December 15, 1791;

Ohio, May 6, 1873; Wyoming, March 6, 1978; Maine, April 27, 1983; Colorado, April 22, 1984; South Dakota, February 21, 1985; New Hampshire, March 7, 1985; Arizona, April 3, 1985; Tennessee, May 23, 1985; Oklahoma, July 10, 1985; New Mexico, February 14, 1986; Indiana, February 24, 1986; Utah, February 25, 1986; Arkansas, March 6, 1987; Montana, March 17, 1987; Connecticut, May 13, 1987; Wisconsin, July 15, 1987; Georgia, February 2, 1988; West Virginia, March 10, 1988; Louisiana, July 7, 1988; Iowa, February 9, 1989; Idaho, March 23, 1989; Nevada, April 26, 1989; Alaska, May 6, 1989; Oregon, May 19, 1989; Minnesota, May 22, 1989; Texas, May 25, 1989; Kansas, April 5, 1990; Florida, May 31, 1990; North Dakota, March 25, 1991; Alabama, May 5, 1992; Missouri, May 5, 1992; Michigan, May 7, 1992; New Jersey, May 7, 1992. Ratification was completed on May 7, 1992. The amendment was subsequently ratified by Illinois on May 12, 1992 and California on June 26, 1992.

CERTIFICATION OF VALIDITY

Publication of the certifying statement of the Archivist of the United States that the amendment had become valid was made on May 18, 1992, F.R. Doc. 92–11951, 57 F.R. 21187. [EDITORIAL NOTE: There is some conflict as to the exact dates of ratification of the amendments by the several States. In some cases, the resolutions of ratification were signed by the officers of the legislatures on dates subsequent to that on which the second house had acted. In other cases, the Governors of several of the States "approved" the resolutions (on a subsequent date), although action by the Governor is not contemplated by article V, which required ratification by the legislatures (or conventions) only. In a number of cases, the journals of the State legislatures are not available. The dates set out in this document are based upon the best information available.]

VerDate Aug 31 2005 11:19 Dec 10, 2007 Jkt 036932 PO 00000 Frm 00033 Fmt 7601 Sfmt 7601
E:\HR\OC\932.CC 932 cprice-sewell on PROD1PC72 with HEARING

VerDate Aug 31 2005 11:19 Dec 10, 2007 Jkt 036932 PO 00000 Frm 00034 Fmt 7601 Sfmt 7601
E:\HR\OC\932.CC 93

PROPOSED AMENDMENTS TO THE CONSTITUTION
NOT RATIFIED BY THE STATES

During the course of our history, in addition to the 27 amendments that have been ratified by the required three-fourths of the States, six other amendments have been submitted to the States but have not been ratified by them. Beginning with the proposed Eighteenth Amendment, Congress has customarily included a provision requiring ratification within seven years from the time of the submission to the States. The Supreme Court in Coleman v. Miller, 307 U.S. 433 (1939), declared that the question of the reasonableness of the time within which a sufficient number of States must act is a political question to be determined by the Congress. In 1789, twelve proposed articles of amendment were submitted to the States. Of these, Articles III–XII were ratified and became the first ten amendments to the Constitution, popularly known as the Bill of Rights. In 1992, proposed Article II was ratified and became the 27th amendment to the Constitution. Proposed Article I which was not ratified is as follows: "ARTICLE THE FIRST "After the first enumeration required by the first article of the Constitution, there shall be one Representative for every thirty thousand, until the number shall amount to one hundred, after which the proportion shall be so regulated by Congress, that there shall be not less than one-hundred Representatives, nor less than one Representative for every forty thousand persons, until the number of Representatives shall amount to two hundred; after which the proportion shall be so regulated by Congress, that there shall not be less than two hundred Representatives, nor more than one Representative for every fifty thousand persons."

Thereafter, in the 2nd session of the Eleventh Congress, the Congress proposed the following article of amendment to the Constitution relating to acceptance by citizens of the United States of titles of nobility from any foreign government. The proposed amendment, which was not ratified by three- fourths of the States, is as follows: Resolved by the Senate and House of Representatives of the United States of America in Congress assembled, two thirds of both houses concurring, That the following section be submitted to the legislatures of the several states, which, when ratified by the legislatures of three fourths of the states, shall be valid and binding, as a part of the constitution of the United States. If any citizen of the United States shall accept, claim, receive or retain any title of nobility or honour, or shall, without the consent of Congress, accept and retain any present, pension, office or emolument of any kind whatever, from any emperor, king, prince or foreign power, such person shall cease to be a citizen of the United States, and shall be incapable of holding any office of trust or profit under them, or either of them. The following amendment to the Constitution relating to slavery was proposed by the 2d session of the Thirty-sixth Congress on

VerDate Aug 31 2005 11:19 Dec 10, 2007 Jkt 036932 PO 00000 Frm 00035 Fmt 7601 Sfmt 7601
E:\HR\OC\932.CC 932 cprice-sewell on PROD1PC72 with HEARING

March 2, 1861, when it passed the Senate, having previously passed the House on February 28, 1861. It is interesting to note in this connection that this is the only proposed (and not ratified) amendment to the Constitution to have been signed by the President. The President's signature is considered unnecessary because of the constitutional provision that on the concurrence of two-thirds of both Houses of

Congress the proposal shall be submitted to the States for ratification. Resolved by the Senate and House of Representatives of the United States of America in Congress assembled, That the following article be proposed to the Legislatures of the several States as an amendment to the Constitution of the United States, which, when ratified by three-fourths of said Legislatures, shall be valid, to all intents and purposes, as part of the said Constitution, viz: "ARTICLE THIRTEEN "No amendment shall be made to the Constitution which will authorize or give to Congress the power to abolish or interfere, within any State, with the domestic institutions thereof, including that of persons held to labor or service by the laws of said State."

A child labor amendment was proposed by the 1st session of the Sixty-eighth Congress on June 2, 1926, when it passed the Senate, having previously passed the House on April 26, 1926. The proposed amendment, which has been ratified by 28 States, to date, is as follows:

JOINT RESOLUTION PROPOSING AN AMENDMENT

TO THE CONSTITUTION OF THE UNITED STATES

Resolved by the Senate and House of Representatives of the United States of America in Congress assembled (two-thirds of each House concurring therein), That the following article is proposed as an amendment to the Constitution of the United States, which, when ratified by the legislatures of three-fourths of the several States, shall be valid to all intends and purposes as a part of the Constitution:

"ARTICLE—.

"**SECTION 1.** The Congress shall have power to limit, regulate, and prohibit the labor of persons under eighteen years of age.

"**SECTION 2.** The power of the several States is unimpaired by this article except that the operation of State laws shall be suspended to the extent necessary to give effect to legislation enacted by the Congress."

An amendment relative to equal rights for men and women was proposed by the 2d session of the Ninety-second Congress on March 22, 1972, when it passed the Senate, having previously passed the House on October 12, 1971. The seven-year deadline for ratification of the proposed amendment was extended to June 30, 1982, by the 2d session of the Ninety-fifth Congress. The proposed amendment, which was not ratified by three-fourths of the States by June 30, 1982, is as follows:

JOINT RESOLUTION PROPOSING AN AMENDMENT

TO THE CONSTITUTION OF THE UNITED STATES

RELATIVE TO EQUAL RIGHTS FOR MEN AND WOMEN

Resolved by the Senate and House of Representatives of the United States of America in Congress assembled (two-thirds of each House concurring therein), That the following article is proposed as an amendment to the Constitution of the United States, which shall be valid to all intents and purposes as part of the Constitution when ratified by the legislatures of three-fourths of the several States within seven years from the date of its submission by the Congress:

VerDate Aug 31 2005 11:19 Dec 10, 2007 Jkt 036932 PO 00000 Frm 00036 Fmt 7601 Sfmt 7601 E:\HR\OC\932.CC 932

"ARTICLE—

"SECTION 1. Equality of rights under the law shall not be denied or abridged by the United States or by any State on account of sex.

"SEC. 2. The Congress shall have the power to enforce, by appropriate legislation, the provisions of this article.

'SEC. 3. This amendment shall take effect two years after the date of ratification."

An amendment relative to voting rights for the District of Columbia was proposed by the 2d session of the Ninety-fifth Congress on August 22, 1978, when it passed the Senate, having previously passed the House on March 2, 1978. The proposed amendment, which was not ratified by three-fourths of the States within the specified seven-year period, is as follows:

JOINT RESOLUTION PROPOSING AN AMENDMENT

TO THE CONSTITUTION

TO PROVIDE FOR REPRESENTATION OF

THE DISTRICT OF COLUMBIA IN THE CONGRESS.

Resolved by the Senate and House of Representatives of the United States of America in Congress assembled (two-thirds of each House concurring therein), That the following article is proposed as an amendment to the Constitution of the United States, which shall be valid to all intents and purposes as part of the Constitution when ratified by the legislatures of three-fourths of the several States within seven years from the date of its submission by the Congress:

71

"ARTICLE—

"SECTION 1. For purposes of representation in the Congress, election of the President and Vice President, and article V of this Constitution, the District constituting the seat of government of the United States shall be treated as though it were a State.

"SEC. 2. The exercise of the rights and powers conferred under this article shall be by the people of the District constituting the seat of government, and as shall be provided by the Congress.

"SEC. 3. The twenty-third article of amendment to the Constitution of the United States is hereby repealed.

"SEC. 4. This article shall be inoperative, unless it shall have been ratified as an amendment to the Constitution by the legislatures of three-fourths of the several States within seven years from the date of its submission."

This ends the Constitution, Amendments and the Bill of Rights. This doesn't just end here. There is so much riding on all these documents. They were written to protect our rights. To protect us from dishonest leaders and authorities, but today it seems no one even knows what they say. Dishonest leaders are trying to rule us. There is espionage, crime of all kinds, murder, theft, torture of all kinds. God help us! We need a leader that loves You God, trust in You, and lets You guide them in guiding us. Our children should be taught this constitution in school. It should be taught in their history classes.

ABORTION THE ULTIMATE MURDER

In exposing the darkness through this book I feel compelled to tell you of another horror and that is abortion. Roe vs Wade a sick law passed by demonic lovers of death and killing. These are women who hate being tied down to a child and who have no concept of what they are doing to their bodies and their lives. A baby is formed in the womb at the time of conception. As my friend **Sherry Desloge**, an RN who serves the community through an RV that allows these women to see their baby in an ultrasound, before they go in the butcher shop to kill their babies says; *"God creates and we conceive and He has given us the gift of life. Science says that it is a live being the minute of conception. The minute that sperm hits the egg and the chromosomes effectively combine 23 of each you have a baby, a human being; it's just very small."* I asked her about the women they come in contact with, how do they approach them before they enter the butcher house and what do they think. She said, *"They are surprised by us being right outside of the abortion clinics. We share the gospel and it is God and the Holy Spirit, they are the ones that will help the women to make the right decision. Ninety-nine percent of the women tell us they are scared and they have no choice. Some have had two days to think about it and others have weeks where they have agonized about this decision and by the time they make the appointment they are ready to get this over with as quickly as possible. They think that it is finally going to be the end of everything, when really it is only the beginning."* **Sherry Desloge** #17

Many women have abortions and they live a good portion of their lives regretting that decision! They have nightmares and can't get over it. Some even commit suicide over it.

Hillary Clinton made the comment *"An unborn person doesn't have any constitutional rights."* April 2016. In that same interview she says, *"I support Roe vs Wade."*

On the other hand Donald Trump according to Lifenews.com: Donald Trump today has issued a call to make permanent the Hyde Amendment that bans almost all federal taxpayer funding of abortions and is credited with **saving the lives of over 1 million Americans from abortion***. Trump's call comes as Hillary Clinton is campaigning to reverse Hyde and force Americans to fund free abortions for women with their tax dollars.*
STEVEN ERTELT SEP 16, 2016 | 9:22AM WASHINGTON, DC # 18

ABORTION

Just a couple days ago, I had to honor of speaking to an abortion doctor as they walked out of the clinic where they had worked for the last time. Through our conversations, he shared with me that he really wanted to tell a short clip of his story. He said he wanted to help people understand how vital our work was at ATTWN.

As a warning, this story contains a very graphic description of an abortion procedure that helped lead to his conversion.

....

אֵל עוֹלָם

"People have asked me why I became a doctor who performed abortions. If I'm honest, the original draw was the money. I didn't have to take call. I didn't have to work any emergencies.

There were no overnights. I walked into the clinic, worked a few hours and walked out with a paycheck for several thousand dollars.

Over time, I convinced myself that I was part of a noble mission to help women in their time of need. After all, if it wasn't for me, these women would be self-aborting and that's what we were trying to prevent.

I never talked about what I did when asked by my colleagues or even family members. They knew I was a doctor and that was really all I disclosed. If I was really helping women, I couldn't figure out why I was ashamed of my work. I felt like I should be proud if I was living the narrative I had worked out in my mind. Yet, the shame was there.

No one in my family dared breach the subject of my employment. All of my immediate family knew, of course. But there were differences in opinion, so everyone stayed silent. Well, almost everyone. One of my close family members started inviting me to church. I went because I was proud of them and of the role they had taken on in ministry. I had grown up in church, but had fallen away from my faith in college. I didn't know what to expect, but surprisingly enjoyed the service. So when they asked me to come again, I agreed, again and again.

One Sunday after church, this particular family member took me to lunch and confronted me about my work. I could tell it made them very uncomfortable, but I really admired their courage. And to be perfectly honest, I felt challenged. I realized during our talk that I had brought shame and embarrassment to my family. I had taken this job because the money enticed me. I wanted to be able to provide for my family with "things." What I realized is that there was no amount of "things" I could buy that would make up for the shame I had caused them.

So then what? I was in a contract with my current employer and I didn't think there was any way I could give up my job. I figured I would just keep doing what I was doing until my contract ran out.

Life changed for me during a 16-17 week abortion. I was performing a D&E procedure and had already pulled off both legs of this small human being. Every once in a while, you begin to pull out the fetus and the majority of the body will come out intact. I began to pull on the torso and the rest of the body came out whole.

74

The arms, head, and torso were all still attached. I was moving the body to the tray for disposal and a slight movement caught my eye. I looked at this tiny chest and saw it moving up and down. Life was outside that woman's womb, even just for a few seconds.

And there I was. I was holding this tiny body. An overwhelming remorse flooded my body. I had violently removed this child's legs while she was still alive. I did that. She felt it. I was the last person to hold her alive, yet I was the person who ended her life. In that moment, I was thankful that she didn't have the ability to open her eyes. I wouldn't have wanted my face to be the first one she would have seen. Now I have hope that the first face she saw was the face of Jesus.

That was when I knew I had to leave, no matter the consequences. I would be breaking my contract and I knew that would be financially devastating. I didn't know if I would be able to work as a doctor again. I honestly didn't know if I would ever be able to recover from what I had done.

I have since left my job and am soon starting a new position at a facility that upholds the sacredness of human life. I have a long way to go. I still have a lot of things to work through, a lot of beliefs that are being challenged. I have a lifetime of healing to do, but knowing that I'm not doing it alone, that I have the support of Abby and her ministry is helping me put one foot in front of the other.

Thank you to everyone who supports this organization. I ask for your prayers during this time and thank you for helping me and people in similar situations find healing and hope."

Abby Johnson CEO/Founder of ATTWN # 19

SECRET SOCIETIES AND TERRORISM

There are several secret societies that are dangerous to our society. Some have been around since the 1700's. I'll name a few here: FED (Federal Reserve Department), Tri-lateral Commission, CFR (Council on Foreign Relations), free Masons; Bilderberg, Illuminati and these are globalists groups that are trying to rule the world not just the United States. The Rockefellers' and Rothschild's' are the biggest contributors to this initiative. The Free Masons say they are God and that there is no god except them. John Kennedy wanted to abolish the FED and he was assassinated. Henry Ford once said, *"It is well enough that people of the nation do not understand our banking and monetary system, for if they did, I believe there would be a revolution before tomorrow morning"* **Henry Ford**   #20

In a recent article, "A Force of One: the Federal Reserve," Chuck Norris makes the claim that the FED is a secret society, "I agree with Judge Andrew Napolitano, who said last week, 'We know more about the CIA than we do about the Federal Reserve. The Federal Reserve is the Freemasonry of government agencies. It is a virtual secret society unto themselves - a group of unelected brokers who hold the value of our dollar in the palms of their hands. This one agency, with its power to raise and lower interest rates, has exercised more control over the economy than any other government body."
Chuck Norris   #21

These exposures could be dangerous to me, so I ask for your prayers!

And let's not forget to mention the Muslim Brotherhood. This is a group of Muslim extremist, jihadist and terrorists. We let these people come over here by the droves. Many are in key positions in the White House. Below is a little portion from their Quran:

Al-Banna's Islam was an all-encompassing one:

"We believe the provision of Islam and its teachings are all inclusive, encompassing the affairs of the people in this world and the hereafter.

And those who think that these teachings are concerning only with the spiritual or ritualistic aspects are mistaken in this believe because Islam is a faith and a ritual, a nation and a nationality, a religion and a state, spirit and deed, holy text and sword...The Glorious Quran...considers [these things] to be the core of Islam and its essence"
Quran (Moaddel 197) #22

Jihad is a radical sect that has interpreted the Quran as endorsing killing of infidels, and holy warfare, usually associated with attacks on innocents. There violence has erupted all over the world. Here we witnessed it first hand on 9/11 when they stole our planes and crashed into the World Trade Centers and destroyed them along with thousands of innocent lives. Then they tried to crash into the White House but a group of brave people on the plane diverted the attack to their own detriment. This plane crashed into a field in Pennsylvania. One more plane crashed into the Pentagon. France has had her share of attacks too. As I just stated it has been worldwide. And we have a President in the White House that will not name the terrorist. It is radical Islamic terrorism!

אֶל עוֹלָם

Radical Islam's kinship with terrorism, and its willingness to use violence as a means to its ultimate ends, is clearly spelled out in a training manual produced by the radical Islamist terror group al Qaeda, whose operatives carried out the 9/11 attacks. This publication candidly says:

"[An] Islamic government would never be established except by the bomb and rifle. Islam does not coincide or make a truce with unbelief, but rather confronts it. The confrontation that Islam calls for with these godless and apostate regimes, does not know Socratic debates, Platonic ideals nor Aristotelian diplomacy. But it knows the dialogue of bullets, the ideals of assassination, bombing, and destruction, and the diplomacy of the cannon and machine-gun. The young came to prepare themselves for Jihad [holy war], commanded by the majestic Allah's order in the holy Koran."

Scholar of Middle East affairs Martin Kramer further describes the goals of radical Islamists:

"The idea is simple: Islam must have power in this world. It is the true religion—the religion of God—and its truth is manifest in its power. When Muslims believed, they were powerful. Their power has been lost in modern times because Islam has been abandoned by many Muslims, who have reverted to the condition that preceded God's revelation to the Prophet Muhammad. But if Muslims now return to the original Islam, they can preserve and even restore their power. That return, to be effective, must be comprehensive; Islam provides the one and only solution to all
questions in this world, from public policy to private conduct. It is not merely a religion, in the
Western sense of a system of belief in God. It possesses an immutable law, revealed by God that deals with every aspect of life and it is an ideology, a complete system of belief about the organization of the state and the world. This law and ideology can only be implemented through the establishment of a truly Islamic state, under the sovereignty of God (May I insert here not our God but Allah their god). The empowerment of Islam, which is God's plan for mankind, is a sacred end."
Discoveringthenetworks.org   A Guide to the political left. #23

I am trying to get this book finished and published before the election so for sake of finishing up I'll not go into detail, but perhaps in a revised addition I will.

There is Exposure other evil things such as the demonic holiday called Halloween. So many millions of people do not even know that they are opening themselves up to this evil. It has been dubbed as a cute little holiday, and little children dress up in costumes and knock on doors, asking for candy. In speaking with real live actual witches, I have learned some things about Halloween. It is a day for dark spirits to come all out, they tell me. They put spells on people and have rituals of killing animals and having human sacrifices. As I mentioned before I may expound more on all these things in a revised edition.

ISLAMIC ATTACKS AND THREATS DURING OBAMA'S PRESIDENCY
ANN-MARIE MURRELL SATURDAY, SEPTEMBER 10, 2011

Here's a list of Islamic terrorist attacks and/or threats of attacks that have occurred on U.S. soil and U.S. military bases since Obama took office in January, 2009.

Oh and just a reminder—although 9/11 happened 8 months after President Bush took office, during his 8-year presidency we never had any other Islamic terrorist attack in the U.S. They knew better.

1. Binghamton, New York — May, 2009
Taliban chief claims responsibility for N.Y. shooting massacre.

2. Bronx, New York — May, 2009
FBI arrest four in alleged plot to bomb Bronx synagogues, shoot down plane

3. Little Rock, Arkansas — June, 2009
Shooting at military recruiting center; 1 dead, 1 wounded; suspect is anti-military Muslim convert

4. New York and Colorado – September 21, 2009
Three men were arrested and charged in the ongoing terror probe centered around New York and Colorado. The three men are Najibullah Zazi, 24; his father Mohammed Wali Zazi, 53; and Ahmad Wais Afzali, 37. When authorities searched Zazi's car, they found a laptop computer that contained "a jpeg image of nine-pages of handwritten notes. Zazi had connections to high levels of al Qaeda.

5. Dallas, Texas — September 22, 2009
A 19-year-old Jordanian man, Hosam Maher Husein Smadi, was arrested on charges he intended to bomb a downtown Dallas skyscraper. Smadi placed what he believed to be a car bomb outside the 60-story Fountain Place office tower, according to a statement from the U.S. attorney's office in Dallas. The decoy device was given to him by an undercover FBI agent.

6. Fort Hood, Texas — November, 2009
Fort Hood massacre: Major Hasan killed 13 service men and women and wounded over 40 others. He has been linked to al-Qaeda.

7. Detroit, Michigan – December, 2009
Northwest 253 passengers tell of thwarted Detroit terror attack.

8. May, 1st, 2010 United States New York City, New York
United States New York's Times Square was evacuated after the discovery of a car bomb.[235] en.wikipedia.org

9. Thwarted attack in November 2010 by 'Christmas tree bomber'
Mohamed Osman Mohamud is accused of plotting to bomb a Portland, Ore., Christmas tree lighting ceremony. www.csmonitor.com

10. Frankfort, Germany United States Military base, March 2011
Islamist terrorists attacked US military base killing two US soldiers. abcnews.go.com

11. New York and DC, September 9, 2011
Islamic terrorists threaten to attack on the 10-year anniversary of 9/11. Both cities on 'high alert' as 'a specific, credible threat' targets New York and Washington. www.foxnews.com

ANN-MARIE MURRELL SATURDAY, SEPTEMBER 10, 2011 #24

אֵל עוֹלָם

Ever since 9/11/01, Americans have been mystified by the motivation of the terrorists of that day. Actually, for many years, Israel has faced regular incidents with terrorists with the same motivation. It is hoped that this essay will help clarify some issues.

Those 19 Muslims of 9/11 are nearly always referred to as "suicide bombers" as are all of them in Israeli incidents. That certainly is the reality of the situation, but it is quite different from what they perceive it to be.

*Yes, to some extent, there were political motivations, and the desire to please their leader, and the responsibility to follow orders. But a much higher motivation exists within extremist Islamic terrorists, a religious motivation. Since around 1970, a small but growing group of aberrant Muslims have been teaching a VERY improper understanding of their religious Koran. Since Muslims all believe that the Koran is the very words of God (Allah, PBUH) Himself, when they are taught bizarre interpretations of the meaning of some sections of it, they come to truly believe that they are REQUIRED to do terrorist acts, against Israel (their "enemy") and the United States (Israel's friend, so their perceived "enemy"). On top of this believed requirement for such acts is the bonus of believing that, having done it (in a specific way), **and gotten killed in the process**, they will immediately go to Paradise (Heaven).*

*The Muslim Koran is much more similar to the Christian Bible than most people realize. **Specifically, the Koran VERY clearly states that suicide, under ANY conditions, is banned and a terrible sin.** An example is in Sura 3, Imram's Family (3.139), "It is not for any soul to die, save by God's permission written down for an appointed time."*

Therefore, from those terrorists' viewpoints, they are DEFINITELY not committing suicide!

C Johnson, Theoretical Physicist, Physics Degree from Univ of Chicago   #25

80

WARS AND RUMORS OF WARS

Mark 13:7, 8 *(7) and when you hear of wars and rumors of wars, do not be alarmed. This must take place, but the end is not yet. (8) For nation will rise against nation, and kingdom against kingdom. There will be earthquakes in various places; there will be famines. These are but the beginning of the birth pains.* **NSV** #26

Ever since the beginning of time there have been wars. As we see above God said there would be. We are living in an imperfect world. Until the Lord Jesus comes back, there will be wars and rumors of wars. When we see imminent danger we do not stand in the street and wait for it to hit, no we run and hide or we fight back. In order to know the truth someone has to tell it right? That's the purpose of this book.

I want to mention our honorable servicemen and servicewomen also for as long as time began they have been around to protect us. I thank God for them all the time. They deserve our honor! This is the only president that I know of in history that just ignores them. Get's off the plane that we tax payers pay for and doesn't even salute them and when he is reminded of it, it is half hearted.

Even the bible speaks of "How can they know without a preacher." Prophets in the Old Testament were sent to warn of things to come.

Matthew 24:3-14 *(3) As he sat on the Mount of Olives, the disciples came to him privately, saying, "Tell us, when will these things be, and what will be the sign of your coming and of the end of the age?" (4) And Jesus answered them, "See that no one leads you astray. (5) For many will come in my name, saying, 'I am the Christ,' and they will lead many astray. (6) And you will hear of wars and rumors of wars. See that you are not alarmed, for this must take place, but the end is not yet. (7) For nation will rise against nation, and kingdom against kingdom, and there will be famines and earthquakes in various places. (8) All these are but the beginning of the birth pains. (9) "Then they will deliver you up to tribulation and put you to death, and you will be hated by all nations for my name's sake. (10) And then many will fall away and betray one another and hate one another. (11)And many false prophets will arise and lead many astray. (12) And because lawlessness will be increased, the love of many will grow cold. (13) But the one who endures to the end will be saved. (14) And this gospel of the kingdom will be proclaimed throughout the whole world as a testimony to all nations, and then the end will come.* **NSV**   #27

Below take a look at some of the wars:

American Revolutionary War	1775-1783
Northwest Indian War	1785-1795
War of 1812	1812-1814
Second Seminole War	1835-1842
Mexican-American War	1846-1848
American Civil War	1861-1865
Great Sioux War of 1876	1876-1877
Spanish–American War	1898-1898
Moro Rebellion	1899-1913
World War I	1917-1918
World War II	1941-1945
Korean War	1950-1953
Viet Nam	1964-1973
Persian Gulf War	1990-1991
Kosovo War	1999-1999
War in Afghanistan	2001- present
Iraq War	2003-2011
War on (ISIS)	2014-present

Wikipedia   #28

Trump earns endorsement of 88 retired generals, admirals

By Nick Gass

The media has done everything they can to portray Donald Trump as a villain. Unfortunately, many people with experience have started publicly backing his message, and acknowledging he could be just the type of leader America needs. According to recent reports, 88 retired U.S. Generals and Admirals wrote an open letter, claiming they support Trump and his "commitment to rebuild our military, to secure our borders, to defeat our Islamic supremacist adversaries and restore law and order domestically."

"As retired senior leaders of America's military, we believe that such a change can only be made by someone who has not been deeply involved with, and substantially responsible for, the hollowing out of our military and the burgeoning threats facing our country around the world," the letter reads.

"For this reason, we support Donald Trump's candidacy to be our next Commander-in-Chief."

Trump was quick to respond to the glowing endorsement. From the beginning, he has thrown his support behind our men and women in uniform.

"It is a great honor to have such amazing support from so many distinguished retired military leaders," Trump commented. "I thank each of them for their service and their confidence in me to serve as commander-in-chief."

"We can only Make America Great Again if we ensure our military remains the finest fighting force in the world, and that's exactly what I will do as president," Trump concluded.

The letter was reportedly organized by Major General Sidney Shachnow, the only survivor of the Holocaust that went on to become a U.S. General. He partnered with Rear Admiral Charles Williams, who received the Legion of Merit.

In his statement, Williams suggested the letter demonstrates that military leaders believe "Donald Trump is more trusted to be commander-in-chief than Hillary Clinton."

"Hillary Clinton has made clear she is running as a staunch defender of the status quo when it comes to the issues facing our military, and she has shown through her foreign policy decisions and her mishandling of classified information that she lacks the judgment to do the job," Lt. Gen. Mike Flynn added in the press release. "Mr. Trump's deep and growing support in the military community and his thoughtful proposals show he's the right person to lead our men and women in uniform."

Politico article: By NICK GASS 09/06/16 06:45 AM EDT   #29

The Most Essential Election Ever

If anyone is still unsure as to who to vote for let me share with you one pastor's: sentiments.

If you're on the Fence about Your Vote, This Pastor Clarifies How the Very Future of America Is at Stake

10:00AM EDT 8/11/2016 DR. JIM GARLOW/SKYLINE CHURCH, SAN DIEGO

אֵל עוֹלָם

1. *The Democratic and Republican party platforms are as different as night and day, in my opinion, as far apart as evil vs. good. The 51-page Democratic platform is the most leftist ever. (I don't care for the "right vs. left" nomenclature. I am far more concerned with "right vs. wrong.") The Democratic platform contains many points which are anti-biblical. (Time does not permit me here to identify what is meant by "anti-biblical," which is covered in my new book Well Versed: Biblical Answers to Today's Tough Issues.) It is thoroughly socialistic (a socialist is a communist without a gun). The 54-page GOP platform is one of the strongest GOP platforms ever. A biblically alert person could be comfortable with almost all of it. Party platforms are a* big issue to me. *Although some "blow off" party platforms, I do not. Nor do many people up and down the ballot who are running for office. This is a serious and very important item. I have a hard copy of both platforms in front of me now. Most people have never checked out what the party platforms say. They should. If a person is not drawn to the "top-of-the-ballot" candidate, they ought to at least consider voting for the candidate attached to the best party platform.*

2. *Analogy #1: Both candidates are flawed. We all know that. But permit me an analogy: As a pastor, I would rather deal with a church attendee who is blatant and brash in his sinning than one who is devious, lying, cunning and deceptive. Both are problematic, but one is easier to deal with than the other. If I were a pastor bringing correction to a parishioner, I would prefer dealing with a "Trump-type" any day over a "Hillary-type." The chances of making progress with the "Trump-type" are many times greater than the "Hillary-type."*

13. *Trump will address the massive government spending. Hillary will expand it above the existing unsustainable debt the U.S. currently is carrying (almost $20 trillion plus unfunded liabilities to Social Security, etc).*

14.   Trump will expose—and I pray, bring down—"the systemic evil" (crony, deceitful, misuse of capitalism) that reigns among many high-dollar lobbyists. Hillary thrives because of them.

15.   Trump will stop the massive overreach of government. Hillary will extend it.

16.   Freedoms come in "threes." Political freedom, economic freedom and religious liberty coexist together. Take one away and the other two will eventually disappear. One cannot exist without the other two. The genius of America is that it had all three, until recently. Trump fully grasps the loss of religious liberty. I have heard him speak on it in person on several occasions. He knows that economic and political freedoms are evaporating. He will reverse that. Hillary will decimate all three.

17.   Every rational person knows the Supreme Court appointments are paramount. Trump has listed 11 superb potential nominees. Hillary's appointments would snuff out the tiny vestige of the three freedoms that are left (mentioned in the statement above).

18.   I make no excuse for wrongdoing or wrongful, hurtful words from either candidate. Candidly, I want King Jesus. He rules in my heart. And yours too, I suspect. And I want Him to rule here—now. But that day is not fully manifested—yet. In the meantime, we prayerfully, carefully navigate this challenging election season, with great concern that above all, we honor our Lord and Savior Jesus Christ in every arena of our lives, including the voting booth. That is my hope. I believe it is yours as well.

10:00AM EDT 8/11/2016 DR. JIM GARLOW/SKYLINE CHURCH, SAN DIEGO *#30*

Modern Day Sodom and Gomorrah

I guess I would be remiss if I didn't speak a moment on another wrong that has been misrepresented by our culture today, and that is the LGBT community. They have come a long way since the closet days. It now is blatantly thrown in our faces with an immense fervor, and we are to accept it! They also are trying to change the very definition of marriage; this has never in the history of the world been a challenge. They are even trying to teach our small children to question God's design for them. This community would have us bow to their wishes and subject our children to imminent danger by allowing men to use the women's restrooms. Scripture tells us God does NOT change, He is the same yesterday, today and forever and when he destroyed an entire society minus Lot and his family, He didn't change His mind today and say I must reform and just be tolerant that I made a mistake. God has NOT changed His mind nor has He made a mistake!

Leviticus 18:22 and 20:13 tell us: 18:22"You shall not lie with a male as with a woman; it is an abomination." 20:13 "If a man lies with a male as with a woman, both of them have committed an abomination; they shall surely be put to death; their blood is upon them." Before you women think you are out of the equation read on. **ESV** #31

Romans 1:26 (26) for this reason (What reason you ask? It's because, they did not give God the honor He deserves or were thankful to Him!) God gave them up to dishonorable passions. For their women exchanged natural relations for those that are contrary to nature; (27) and the men likewise gave up natural relations with women and were consumed with passion for one another, men committing shameless acts with men and receiving in themselves the due penalty for their error. (28) And since they did not see fit to acknowledge God, God gave them up to a debased mind to do what ought not to be done. (29) They were filled with all manner of unrighteousness, evil, covetousness, malice. They are full of envy, murder, strife, deceit, maliciousness. They are gossips, (30) slanderers, haters of God, insolent, haughty, boastful, inventors of evil, disobedient to parents, (31) foolish, faithless, heartless, ruthless. (32) Though they know God's righteous decree that those who practice such things deserve to die, they not only do them but give approval to those who practice them. **ESV** #32

II Peter 2 4-10 *(4) For if God did not spare angels when they sinned, but cast them into hell and committed them to chains of gloomy darkness to be kept until the judgment; (5) if he did not spare the ancient world, but preserved Noah, a herald of righteousness, with seven others, when he brought a flood upon the world of the ungodly; (6) if by turning the cities of Sodom and Gomorrah to ashes he condemned them to extinction, making them an example of what is going to happen to the ungodly; (7) and if he rescued righteous Lot, greatly distressed by the sensual conduct of the wicked (8) (for as that righteous man lived among them day after day, he was tormenting his righteous soul over their lawless deeds that he saw and heard); (9) then the Lord knows how to rescue the godly from trials, and to keep the unrighteous under punishment until the day of judgment, (10) and especially those who indulge in the lust of defiling passion and despise authority.* **ESV** #33

For time sake please read the others. I Timothy 1:10 and I Corinthians 6:9

All Lives Matter

As I was finishing this book and was ready to have it published, God said you are not through. I went to bed and on the way to church He began to download to me what He wanted me to do to finish completely. The Father downloads things to me and I write them down. Here and now I add this chapter and then the summation.

I live in Charlotte, NC and we have been through some very unsettling things as I was wrapping up my book. Rioting in the streets, killings, hate being spewed violently! This all came as a result of an African American police shooting an African American. People were asking in this protest to show the video of what happened. If you know anything about court hearings you do not submit evidence before a hearing. It can skew the prosecution and the outcome can be disastrous for the hearing. I have been a juror during a trial and the first thing they tell you is you are not allowed to talk to anyone about the case. It can cause a mistrial. None of this should have come out now. Because of this, now the protestors think they can always do this. People who have multiple rap sheets usually scream the loudest!

Black Lives Matter, excuse me, but the last time I looked there were Chinese, Vietnamese, Blacks, Whites, Israelis', Hispanics, and Muslims all over this planet. I think that means ALL lives matter! This is all a smoke screen to divert our attention from what really matters! That is we protect our citizens, protect our police, and protect us from all harm from outsiders that want us dead! People need jobs; we need to build that wall, medical care, food and much more! This is what is most important and to obey God rather than man!

My prayer is that this city would become united and that peace would reign in our hearts and that we would begin to love one another, and to help each other through all kinds of crisis.

Summary

I want to sum up everything that I have written or have listed from others comments. I will be going back to the beginning.

To recap a little, there has always been discord from the beginning of time. Remember the story of Cain and Abel this was the first murder ever recorded. This was between brothers. It was done all in the name of jealousy. You see that is ultimately where it all comes from Satan was jealous of God, Cain was jealous of Abel and so on and so on until now. The American leaders are so jealous of one another that one might get to be this or that and they may lose, so they start killing off the so called enemy. Beware of that jealous bug! Then you have those who need sympathy so much they will talk about you to the whole world. These people who do the gossiping can somehow always come out smelling like a rose. Then if that is not enough then we have sexual sins. Sex outside of marriage, adultery, sodomites, pedophiles and I could go on, but I think you get the point.

Next here comes the media to stir the big pot! The commercials' on television are getting more risqué. It is the same as the old story about the frog you put into water lukewarm to start, and then gradually increasing the temperature until the frog is boiled to death. Over the years we have allowed more and more evil to creep in until now we are drowning in it and are trying to jump out of the boiling water. America has found herself in the middle of the greatest crisis ever and if we do not turn down the heat we will be annihilated!

I started, talking first about the settlers. They were seeking a place to worship God as they felt they should and the constitution allowed this to happen. I thank God they came here and we do have that freedom to worship, even though some do not feel as we may feel. The freedom is there. I think about Jesus telling His disciples that if they are not against me they are for me. He was answering there complaint that some were healing in His name. Jesus was not advocating sin.

Then we had the names of all the Presidents. I think of the verse that says, **Proverbs 21:1** *"The king's heart is a stream of water in the hand of the LORD; he turns it wherever he will." (NSV)* #34

Ultimately God is always in charge. I think He wants us to ask Him to move on our behalf.

Next I talked about slavery, how awful that people would be used as chattel! Many races have been used this way from biblical times and still even today. This is so barbaric that some leaders could do such a thing and get by with it. I thank God for men like Abraham Lincoln, and Newt Knight who both stood up for this injustice.

Wall of Separation, there is no such thing in the constitution! The founding fathers knew that big government may try to come in and again put us in that bondage we were in when the settlers arrived. Government was tailored and not allowed to interfere with the free expression of a person's religion, and that the government would never interfere with matters of the church. So a liberal mindset wanted to change the meaning but the conservative that doesn't want change made sure it didn't happen. Praise God that the Founding Fathers were guided by God to make a provision for this fiasco!

Abortion the most horrible heinous act perpetrated on mankind. Some of our leaders have made comments such as: an unborn baby doesn't have a constitutional right to be born. The devil has also perpetrated a lie to the women that are pregnant that it is a glob of tissue and that they can fix their problem easily. I feel for the heart of the woman who finds herself in this position, and yes there is a fix and it is NOT abortion! It is called adoption. I have a brother who will tell you he is so grateful to God that his mother gave him up. He was much loved and had a wonderful life with his adopted parents.

We have secret societies and terrorism that are so entrenched in hierarchy that the normal person feels they have no power to do anything. Fear grips a society and we need to be reminded that they are not above the law and fight for our rights like our founding fathers did.

I know the next subject has been a very controversial one. LGBT (lesbian, gay, bi-sexual, transgender) in case you didn't know. My heart does go out to these folks who also are being blinded by the devil. I feel that a lot of them were not taught by their parents as to what true love is and that it is between one man and one woman. Perhaps they were mistreated and felt that that member of the same sex understood them better than anyone else. If you are an LGBT individual God loves you and you can come out of this wrong lifestyle.

This election is an extremely pivotal one. Without pointing fingers, let me just say a Presidential leader should be one that is honest and doesn't lie at the drop of a hat. Doesn't steal, cheat, and doesn't put our country in jeopardy. They should be an individual of high integrity. They should always be strong in protection of our military and our police forces.
This person should put their citizen's protection above any other countries. They should support the clergy and the rights of Christians who are the backbone of this nation. All unborn babies should be protected by the leader of a free nation. Our military would be protected and honored by our Commander and Chief!

God help us and give us a leader that obeys you and your commandments! The truth has been exposed and now it is up to you to take action on these truths. What has been exposed here is truth and may that truth carry on God's purpose for His country! God bless the USA!

WORK SITED SOURCES

Historyofmedicine.com   #1

© Duane A. Cline 1999 The Pilgrims and Plymouth colony   Rootsweb.ancestory.com   #2

National Humanities Center   #3

Encyclopedia Virginia   #4

http://americanhistory.about.com/od/uspresidents/tp/presidential_scandals.htm #5

Clinton Mafia by Charles Krauthammer #6

By Deroy Murdock October 2, 2015 | 8:50pm   #7

New American Standard Bible   NAS   #8

New American Standard Bible   NAS #9

History.com   #10

By (James R. Kelly Jr.)   #11

David Barton-Wallbuilders   #12

by (IrishMike 2009) #13

2011 RussP.us) #14

David Barton (Wall Builders)2001
http://www.wallbuilders.com/libissuesarticles.asp?id=123   #15

http://www.allabouthistory.org/separation-of-church-and-state-in-the-constitution-faq.htm   #16

The Constitution   pages

SHERRY DESLOGE RN   #17

STEVEN ERTELT SEP 16, 2016 | 9:22AM   WASHINGTON, DC #18

Abby Johnson CEO/Founder of ATTWN # 19

Henry Ford #20

Chuck Norris #21

Quran #22

Discoveringthenetworks.org A Guide to the political left.   #23

ANN-MARIE MURRELL SATURDAY, SEPTEMBER 10, 2011   #24

 C Johnson Theoretical Physicist, Physics Degree from Univ. of Chicago   #25

New Standard Version NSV #26

New Standard Version NSV # 27

Wikipedia   #28

Politico article: By NICK GASS 09/06/16 06:45 AM EDT   #29

10:00AM EDT 8/11/2016 DR. JIM GARLOW/SKYLINE CHURCH, SAN DIEGO #30

English Standard Version ESV   #31

English Standard Version ESV   #32

English Standard Version ESV   #33

New Standard Version NSV   #34

אֵל עוֹלָם   **El Olam - Everlasting God**

Addendums

"I believe that the next half century will determine if we will advance the cause of civilization, or revert to the horrors of brutal paganism."
President Theodore Roosevelt (1858-1919)

"The congress of the United States approves and recommends to the people, the Holy Bible...for use in schools."
Congress of the United States (1781).

It cannot be emphasized to strongly or too often that this great nation was founded, not by religionist, but by Christians; not on religions, but on the gospel of Jesus Christ! For this very reason people of other faiths have been afforded asylums, prosperity and freedom of worship here.
Patrick Henry (1736-1799) Distinguished American Statesman

"Our laws and institutions must necessarily be based upon and embody the teachings of the Redeemer of mankind. It is impossible that it should be otherwise; and in this sense and to this extent our civilization and our institutions are empathetically Christian."
United States Supreme Court 1892 Church of the Holy Trinity vs United States

"The fear of God is the beginning of wisdom and its consummation is everlasting felicity."
William Samuel Johnson, Signer of the Constitution, Political and Educational Leader.

"A more beautiful or precious moral of ethics I have never seen; it is a document in proof that I am a real Christian; that is to say, a disciple of the doctrines of Jesus."
Thomas Jefferson 1743-1826 3rd President of the United States.

"The fundamental basis of this nation's laws was given to Moses on the mount."
Harry S Truman 1884-1972 33rd President of the United States.

"The foundations of our society and our government rest so much on the teachings of the Bible that it would be difficult to support them if faith in these teachings would cease to be practically universal in our country."
Calvin Coolidge

"Of the many influences that have shaped the United States into a distinctive nation and people, none may be said to be more fundamental and enduring than the Bible."
Ronald Reagan

"The propitious smiles of Heaven can never be expected on a nation that disregards the eternal rules of order and right, which heaven itself has ordained."
George Washington

"We recognize no sovereign but God, and no King but Jesus!"
John Adams

"The reason that Christianity is the best friend of government is because Christianity is the only religion that changes the heart."
Thomas Jefferson

There are so many more quotes, but I wanted to share a few with you, that show we were created as a Christian Nation.

www.ingramcontent.com/pod-product-compliance
Lightning Source LLC
Chambersburg PA
CBHW070213290526
45789CB00002B/982